Thank you very much!,
Author,
Melvina Gray
12 / 2017

Combat Related PTSD

THE WILLIE GRAY STORY

A True Story

By: Melvina Gray

Some of the names in this story have been changed for identity protection purposes.
Combat Related PTSD: The Willie Gray Story

Self-Published by Melvina Gray

ISBN Thirteen
978-1481134651
ISBN Ten
1481134655

Cover art provided by Yobro10 and Pixattitude – License purchased at www.dreamstime.com

Printed in the United States of America

Combat Related PTSD

THE WILLIE GRAY STORY

Dedication

I dedicate this book to my beloved husband, Willie Gray as an honor of his love, life, and memory. Thank you for having a strong fighting spirit, which helped me to stay strong. Knowing you, you probably are smiling down at me right now for wanting to inspire, encourage, and empower others who are struggling with PTSD.

You were a strong soldier and I admired you for your great fight for life. I truly believe that God looked beyond your faults here on earth and saved your soul for the kingdom. I will forever keep your spirit alive by honoring the memories of you. You are missed and still loved very much. Your spirit will forever be with us until we meet again in our eternal home. I pray your soul forever rests in peace. Love you!

Melvina

Acknowledgements

First, and foremost, I would like to thank God, the most high for continuously guiding and sustaining my life throughout all my endeavors.

I want to personally thank and give special acknowledgement to my dearest friend, Yvette Scott (Darlene) for being an extraordinary person in my life and a great Godmother to my son. It has been an honor and a privilege to call you my friend for over thirty years. I pray for many more years.

You have always had a special place in my heart and together we have always shared a special unique bond. Our friendship means more to me than you will ever know. I have always felt comfortable talking with you. You always listened to me, even if it took half the night for me to express my feelings. Though distance separates us by not living in the same city and state, I know you are always there for me. Thanks for encouraging me not to quit. You are truly the wind beneath my wings!

To my son Kevon Gray (Jamar), thank you for being a wonderful son and for providing technical support with my computer issues. I love you son and I am so proud of you. To my son Curtis and Tara Webb (Lee and Judy), I love you too and I appreciate your support and encouragement to write this book. I also extend my thanks to all of those who played a special role in our lives with prayer, support, and encouragement.

Love Melvina

INTRODUCTION

The purpose of my story is to convey my remarkable life experiences and challenges living with my husband who struggled with PTSD (Post-Traumatic Stress Disorder) as a result of fighting on the battlefield in the Vietnam War. It is my goal to help other families who are living with someone who may have PTSD by helping them to recognize some of the signs and symptoms.

I believe that some people may not be aware of such behaviors, as I was unaware of my husband's for a long time. It is my opinion that PTSD sufferers may be more fortunate physically and psychologically if they receive help at the early stages of the disorder which can result in a more functional life. Although it may be difficult for PTSD sufferers to seek the proper help, continue to encourage them to do so anyway.

It is my desire to take the tragic death of my husband, who struggled through the turmoil from severe Post Traumatic Stress Disorder, and turn it into something positive. PTSD had taken a great toll on his mind and body and eventually led to other health problems, such as depression and many more.

The message in my story tells some of the things I did in order to survive while trying to provide a supportive environment for my husband during the tumultuous obstacles he faced. In my opinion, I believe that it would help greatly if you take your love one to a medical practice that is knowledgeable with the condition and who is able to properly diagnose and treat the condition thoroughly. I believe the pain, stress, and frustrations of living with someone who has PTSD are at times unexplainable. From my experience with my husband, I truly believe that mental wounds never completely heal. Due to my husband struggling from the battle of PTSD, the disease dramatically impacted on our lives. If I had never found out the cause of my husband's actions, then I probably would have left and ended our marriage negating his actions to the fact that he was simply a mean, hateful, selfish and crazy man. I believe having the support of family and friends can make a great difference in many lives.

I pray my story touches the hearts of everyone who is affected by PTSD, and that my message will be beneficial. It may help some to even see it in a different perspective than I did. It is my desire that society can come to grasp with the realization of this disorder that will eliminate the criticisms, stigmatizing, belittling and judgmental behaviors of others.

On a personal note, I believe that when we see a military veteran dressed in uniform or not, we should honor them by at least saying hello and thanking them for the ultimate sacrifice in serving our country by risking their lives for our freedom: even those who may be on the street homeless. Let's not walk by or ignore them as if they don't exist. Make them feel good and appreciated.

My husband use to always say that no one knew all he'd gone through in Vietnam. I say, no one knew all he went through from day to day living with the memories. Many soldiers are at war today continuing to shed their blood and dying fighting a great battle against world evils for us. I believe that many soldiers have returned home with their traumatic stories that continue to haunt and torment them like it did my husband: More or less, bringing the war back home with them.

I am certain that there are many families who have been torn apart and some who have died never knowing that they had been struggling with PTSD. I urge you not to give up too easily on your loved ones. For all who are in the fight with this disease, please try to stay strong and stay encouraged. I pray and hope that others will find strength from my strength. *(I wrote this book according to my own memory. This is how I recall the events during the times with me and my husband.)*

Combat Related PTSD

THE WILLIE GRAY STORY

A True Story

By: Melvina Gray

Chapter 1

This man is about to kill my husband.

That was the only thought running through my head when, after pulling up at a gas station, Willie decided to pick a fight. Willie was driving and he and another man were trying to reach the same gas pump at the same time. Willie lost by a few seconds but decided to let the man know how he felt about it.

Willie got out his car and said to the man that he was wrong for pulling up at that pump first. I tried to tell him that the man had the right of way and Willie yelled at me to shut up. Willie kept talking and said to the man that some niggers don't know how to act. When he said that, the man came angrily toward him with one of his fists balled up ready to swing. I yelled out to the man pleading with him not to hit my husband because he was not well.

The man stopped in his tracks and said to me that I'd better take Willie somewhere and get him well before someone hurt him, because he was about to knock Willie out.

I was relieved when the ordeal was over, but I could only wonder at the actions of my husband. Acting belligerent and irritable at home was one thing. Acting that way in public where someone would surely fight back was another. He needed to know that he couldn't do that, especially when his wife and son were with him.

I told Willie that he could've gotten all of us hurt by acting the way he did. Willie just brushed it all off like it was nothing and said that if the man had put his hands on him, he was going to pull out his gun and shoot him. I told him that the man could have had him in a position where he wouldn't be able to get his gun. All I could do was encourage him not to do that ever again. I knew what I said went through one ear and out the other. I knew he would likely do it again. All I could do was pray.

It would be some time before I realized that his behavior was a result of the time he'd spent in Vietnam during the war. What enveloped him in the war was never dealt with back then, and it gradually brought us to this devastating point. There are many other raw memories that P.T.S.D. is responsible for, but you will read those as you go through the book. I'm recounting these memories because Willie can't. A lot of these memories are painful, and all are deeply personal, but they need to be told. Some things may not be written in the correct order that they happened, but my intent is to focus on the P.T.S.D. and how it affected my husband and our family. I'm hoping that this book will help other families in a similar situation.

The first time I met Willie, it was the weekend of my birthday. I was celebrating at a club in Decatur, GA on a Friday night in October 1989. Two of my close friends, Annie and Annette and I made plans to celebrate. We met at the club for happy hour after getting off from work.

We sat at a table near the dance floor, talking, laughing, eating, drinking, occasionally taking to the dance floor and having a good time. Later that night, our waiter came over and said that there was a gentleman sitting at the bar who'd offered to purchase each of us drinks. We were shocked but delighted. Our desire to find out who this admirer was, led to the waiter pointing to an average looking man, medium build, with dark skin and glasses.

Annette told the waiter to tell the man that we appreciated the gesture and I added that he should tell him that I'll consider that a birthday drink for me. Moments later, the waiter came back to our table and told us that the gentleman told us to order whatever drinks we wanted and he would pick up the tab.

As the night went on, a man selling roses in the club brought a rose wrapped in plastic and presented it to me. He said that it was from a secret admirer wishing me a happy birthday. Some how deep inside I knew it was from the same gentleman that bought us drinks.

"Tell him thanks," I replied.

Not long after that, the gentleman finally came over to our table. He greeted us and to me he asked, "Could I take the birthday girl out on the dance floor?"

I was reluctant, but I took his hand anyway and we danced three songs non-stop to the music. It wasn't until after we got back to my table that he told me his name was Willie.

"My name is Melvina," I shared extending my hand.

My friends introduced themselves. Willie asked if he could sit with us. Hesitantly we told him yes. Willie spent most of the time conversing with me. I really didn't care to share much because I really wasn't interested in meeting anyone; I just wanted to enjoy my birthday.

"Wow, it is getting late," Annette, said.

"Yeah, it is already 1:00 am," Annie added.

"Willie, we are leaving. It was nice meeting you and thank you again for everything," I said as we walked away leaving Willie sitting at the table alone.

We walked slowly to our cars and suddenly heard a man's voice behind us say, "Hey ladies." We looked back and saw Willie. He asked us if we would like to go and get some breakfast. The broad smile on his face widened after we agreed.

Surprisingly, we had a wonderful time at Waffle House, eating, talking, and laughing. After we were done and ready to leave the restaurant, Willie asked me if he could follow me home to make sure I got home safely. I told him flat out N-O! He then asked me for my phone number. Since he treated us with food and drinks, I decided to at least give him my work number. I wanted to make sure he didn't follow me home, so we left the parking lot after Willie did.

The following Monday morning, Willie called me at work and invited me to lunch. I declined because I had already planned to go to lunch with my co-workers. But Willie was persistent. He called my job everyday for about two weeks. A part of me had begun to regret giving him my number at all. Finally, I gave in and told him that I would have lunch with him. From that day forward, he continued picking me up for lunch almost every day before he started his evening work shift. Needless to say, I didn't have too much time to go out for lunch with my co-workers anymore

16

unless Willie just couldn't make it that day for some reason.

During one of our lunch hours, he convinced me to give him my home number. He said he wanted to take me out and do different things since we were both off work on the weekends. I gave him my number, but I refused to tell him where I lived.

For the next two months we dated and focused on getting to know each other. We both had a child from previous relationships. He had a daughter named Linda and I had a son named Lee.

My son, Lee, had left town the latter part of December. He'd gone off to boot camp where he was stationed at the New Jersey Army base for six months. When I told Willie that my son had left, he really started nagging me about coming over. It had been nearly three months, so I gave in and let him come over. Of course I called my friends to let them know he would be visiting me. When he arrived I teasingly told Willie that my friends knew of his visit; that I had the police department on speed dial and that my home security alarm was activated. After our initial laughter, he asked why I felt the need to do all that. I simply told him that I felt uneasy about him being at my place for the first time. That night, we talked and watch TV for a couple hours and after that he left.

A few days later, Willie invited me to go with him to a New Year's Eve party in downtown Atlanta. I allowed him to pick me up from home. We had a very nice time. After arriving back at my place around one in the morning, Willie asked me could he come in for a while. I replied no.

Instead, I allowed him to kiss me on the cheek and he went on home.

We continued to date a lot. Willie would always be the first to plan things for us to do on the weekends. His desire to spend time together led to my spending less time around my friends. Although I missed hanging out with my friends, Willie was extremely nice with a very loving heart and I enjoyed spending time with him. I could tell that Willie's feelings were progressing at a rate much faster than mine. He seemed to be getting serious feelings for me, but I was simply enjoying his friendship.

In February 1990, my friends, Annette, Annie, Cathy, and I were getting ready for a weekend trip to New Orleans for Mardi Gras. They all met me at my apartment so that we could travel in one car. As we were loading up the car trunk with our luggage, Willie drove up. I'd told him the time of our departure a few weeks before we were scheduled to leave. I was surprised to see him there.

"Why are you not at work?" I asked.

He replied, "I took a little break so I could see that you all got on the highway okay.

As I was loading one of the bags, Willie grabbed my hand, put some cash into it and told me to take it and have a good time. I tried giving him the money back but he wouldn't take it. He was so generous.

My friends and I returned from the trip and, Willie came by to see how everything went. I let him stay long enough to hear about what happened during the trip then I asked him to leave because I was tired and needed to unwind alone.

Although Willie and I spent a lot of time together, I still considered him a good friend. It was clear he seemed to be looking for more than just to be a friend. I often suggested we slow things down, as the relationship appeared to be moving quite fast.

It wasn't long into the relationship that Willie started to show signs of jealousy and possessiveness toward me, to the point that I would become more paranoid around him. During one intense moment, I told him that I regretted the day I met him and the day I gave him my phone number and address.

Even though I would get frustrated with him many times, I knew that overall he had a big heart. As time continued to pass, Willie and I spent a lot of time together. It wasn't long before we were in a serious relationship, whether I was willing to admit it or not. The progression of our relationship brought forth many conversations. One in particular was about us having children. He told me that he could not father children because he was sterile. I asked him what made him sterile, and Willie said that during his time spent on the battlefield in Vietnam, he had been exposed to chemicals that caused him to be sterile.

Out of curiosity, I asked him what kind of chemicals made him sterile. He said that the effect of the Agent Orange and other herbicides used during his tour in Vietnam caused his sterilization. I told him that I wanted to know more about this Agent Orange.

I'd never heard of Agent Orange, but even with his explanation, I wanted him to show me proof, documents stating his sterilization. Willie later showed me documents that provided evidence that he really was sterile. He was telling the truth after all.

As time passed, my feelings for Willie continued to grow. I am not sure when or how it happened, but I had to admit I was in love with Willie. Our whirlwind courtship had blossomed into a full-fledged relationship. Our relationship was headed in a positive direction, but every so often Willie would show sides of himself that puzzled me. Love is very powerful and emotional. Willie Gray taught me just how powerful love was.

I got off work one Friday evening in late February and stopped by K-mart to do a little shopping. By the time I arrived home it was dark outside. I got out of my car and started taking bags out of the trunk when I heard a male's voice behind me say, 'hello'. It nearly scared me to death. I looked back and saw that it was Willie. I realized that his car had been parked in between two other cars so I wouldn't see him.

He asked me why I was just getting from work. I lashed out at him and asked what it looked like to him. He saw the bags in my hands. I was way too upset because I wasn't used to a man asking me of my whereabouts. I, in turn, asked him why he wasn't at work. He replied coolly that he'd just decided to get off early.

I told Willie that he should've never shown up at my apartment unannounced. I felt like he was trying to see if I was with someone else. He asked me if I needed help bringing the bags into my home. I told him no because I didn't like that way he just behaved. I told him it was over and to get back in his car and leave. He accused me of having another man in my apartment since I wouldn't let him go in.

After Willie made that statement, I told him if he came back to my apartment, I was going to call the police. Willie left because he saw that I was serious.

A couple hours later he called to tell me that he was very sorry and asked if I would accept his apology. I told him that I had to think about it and hung the phone up on him. Thirty minutes later, he called asking me did I want to go out to eat. I told him no and that he should stay wherever he was because I didn't want to be bothered with him acting foolish. It was very difficult for Willie to accept 'no' as an answer from me. Willie called me back again, but I refused to answer the phone.

The next morning Willie called and I finally answered the phone. He repeatedly asked me to go out with him that evening for dinner and a movie. I didn't go out with him, but I did accept his apology. I stressed again that he did not have the right to just drop by my apartment whenever he felt like it.

Willie continuously pleaded for me to take him back. One day I finally gave in and started seeing him again. He picked me up that evening for dinner and a movie. We had a nice time, but that wasn't enough to make me forget why we had broken up.

Willie's insecurities gave me very little breathing room because he required a lot of my time. One night, I heard my telephone ringing as I stepped out of the shower. I ran to answer it and was out of breath as a result. It was Willie. He asked why I was breathing so hard and then accused me of having another man in my apartment. I told him the reason I was out of breath; he didn't believe me and called me a liar. I was so frustrated that I couldn't even get my point across. I slammed the phone down on the receiver.

I laid there all night trying to understand this man and why he was behaving in the manner that he was. Willie's charm gave much credibility to his apology whenever he had upset me. Only time would tell how long we would last, but I knew in my heart I loved him.

In mid-summer of 1990, Willie invited me to go with him to South Florida to visit some of his cousins. It was a wonderful trip and we had a great time, but it was the traveling back home that tainted the good memories of the trip. We had been conversing nicely about the happenings on the trip and I think I might've given him some information pertaining to the direction of travel. Then all of a sudden, Willie snapped at me for no reason at all. I asked him what was wrong and what I'd said to make him go off on me like that. He told me not to ask any questions.

I just kept asking him what was wrong. But it was as if he couldn't answer me, nor could he stand listening to anything that came out of my mouth. Willie got so angry that he stopped the car on a dark country road in Valdosta, Georgia and got out. He told me if I said another word, he was going to walk or catch a ride to a bus station to get back home. He made it clear that he didn't want to ride any further with me, so he started walking.

I was at my wits end. I didn't know what to do. This had never happened before. All I could do was to beg him to get back in the car. He had to because I surely didn't know the way back home and I didn't want to leave him out there alone.

I was afraid, thinking that something could happen to us out there. As he walked on the dark side of the road, I drove slowly alongside him pleading with him to get into the car. Willie finally got in the car after an hour-long ordeal. He was still angry for some reason. I couldn't figure out what had just happened. He seemingly had a moment of insanity, but I didn't dare open my mouth to ask again.

I couldn't help but think how badly I needed to get this man completely out of my life. I began praying, asking God to place in Willie's mind the fact that he needed to leave me alone. I thought that it might be easier for God to do the dirty work since I had tried and failed.

After that terrible episode, I didn't know how long it would be before God answered my prayer, so I started paying closer attention to Willie's behavior. I determined that he had a real serious split personality. It was unbelievable how his rants became more frequent.

A few weeks later, another incident occurred while we were driving down Interstate 20 headed back to Atlanta. We had attended a friend of mine's wedding anniversary in Charleston, SC. We actually had a lovely time, until he suddenly snapped at me saying that I was driving too slowly. He asked if I thought I was driving in a funeral procession. I asked him, what he meant, since I was driving the speed limit. He told me to stop the car if I couldn't drive any faster adding that he wasn't going to take my "mess".

I asked, 'what mess?'

"Stop the car!" he yelled.

I drove to the next exit and pulled into the store parking lot that was next to a restaurant and hotel. Willie went inside the store and bought a pack of cigarettes. When he came out of the store, he looked into the car and asked why I was still there. He told me that he was not riding any further with me. I shook my head and asked God to please have mercy on me.   I was at a loss again as to why all of this was happening.

I watched Willie walk over to the restaurant, sit down at the counter, and order something to eat. I droved the car over and parked near the door so when he came out, he would see me. I was afraid to get out of the car to join him thinking that he might snap at me again. I stayed in the car and watched him through the window.

When he came out the restaurant, he saw that I was out there and he told me that I might as well go on back home because he was not going with me. He said that he'd get home the best he could; that he'd stay at the hotel nearby. He took his luggage out of the car and told me to leave. I was distraught because I knew I didn't do anything wrong, yet the least little thing would set him off.

I started up my car and left him. I was able to leave this time because I was in a location that I knew. Deep down inside, I was really worried about Willie. I didn't know what was wrong with him, so there was nothing I could do.

I called the hotel the next day to check up on him. The receptionist told me that he'd just checked out and had left in a taxicab. I assumed that he'd get dropped off at a bus station in order to get back home. Willie called me the next day late in the evening accusing me of leaving him stranded and treating him like a motherless child. I asked him what he was talking about because he was the one that told me to leave. After I knew he made it home safely, I just politely told him to leave me alone and then I hung up the phone.

Willie was always the one to start the heated arguments and then blame me. I remember telling him that I just couldn't figure him out. He responded that it wasn't meant for me to figure him out.

I told my friends Annie and Cathy about the weekend incident just in case he decided to go berserk again and do something to harm me. I prayed earnestly that Willie wouldn't call or come by anymore. I thought about changing my phone number but realized that wouldn't do any good because he could call me at work.

The following week, he showed up at my job early. I spotted his car in the parking lot and pulled up right beside him. I asked why he was there. He told me that he needed to talk to me. He wanted me to know how sorry he was.

I fell for his charm, yet again, and it wasn't long before we were back together. It wasn't long after getting back together that he threw another temper tantrum. This time it happened at a restaurant over dinner. All of a sudden he started bickering with me because I asked him a simple question. It was so bad that patrons started to notice. I was so embarrassed.

Willie left the restaurant without eating his meal. I stayed at the table until I was finished. Willie came back inside; small specks of cigarette butts were on his shirt. He picked up the tab and told me that he was ready to leave. I didn't ask any question, I just got up and followed him out.

During the ride back home, I tried to piece together this stranger's way of thinking. He'd gone far from the sweet, considerate man that I'd first met, and turned into this person that I hardly knew. From that point, I really became more careful of what I said or did around Willie. Sometimes, he was like a walking time bomb ready to explode over the least little thing I said to him or did. He always had to be the loudest, get the last word, and be right all the time. Only God knew the true identity of the man I brought into my life because I certainly didn't. But what I did know was that I loved him, and that was what kept me in the relationship.

Chapter 2

One Friday night, Willie stopped by my apartment after work for dinner. As we dined, he asked me what time I'd gotten home because he called me around 5:15 that afternoon but I wasn't at home. I told him that I got off work at my regular time of 4:30 and didn't get home until 6:00.

Willie asked why I took so long and he accused me of stopping off to meet another man. I got up from the table and asked him to leave. As he headed toward the door, he mumbled something to the effect that I told him a lie, which made me even more upset.

At this point, I was tired of him making these false accusations toward me. Out of anger, I threw my shoe at him as he walked down the corridor toward his car.

Willie looked back and saw how I was carrying on and he had the nerve to ask me what my problem was. I told him that he should've known very well that he was my problem. I yelled out to him not to ever step foot back inside my apartment ever again. After that incident, Willie stayed away for two weeks. He didn't even call. I was hoping that I had gotten rid of him for good this time.

I should've known after two weeks had passed that Willie would try to contact me. He showed up at my job's parking lot again one morning. I asked what he was doing there. At first he did not say anything. He just hung his head down. Like other times, he apologized and asked how he could make it up to me. I told him right then that I didn't want to have anything to do with him. At that point, I was trying to enjoy my freedom without talking or seeing him. I declined and went inside the building to go to work. He left, but not for good. A few days later, Willie started the cycle of constantly pleading for us to get back together and apologizing for his behavior. Because of my deep love for him, I continued the cycle of giving in to him.

Since meeting Willie, I'd only told Annie and Cathy what the real deal was between Willie and me. I never told any of my family members and other friends the bad side of our relationship. I was very secretive about the pain I was experiencing with him. I would always try to wear a smile on my face. I wanted people to think that I had a perfect relationship. I never said an unkind word about Willie to anyone, even though I told Annie, and Cathy about some of the things he used to do and they would sometimes just laugh thinking it was funny. I figured since he wasn't allowing me too much phone time with my friends and family, at least they should believe I had a good reason to not spend much time with them anymore. This front that I put on was the only thing that kept me halfway sane with this insane man.

And while I call him insane, the truth is I really did love him. We were spending more time together and my feelings grew stronger every day. At some point, I realized I loved him and wanted the relationship to work.

We went on spending more and more time together. Then one day, he surprised me and proposed at a restaurant. I told him that I had to think about it. He asked several times over the next few weeks until I decided to say yes.

When Willie and I got married, it was at the courthouse in Charleston, SC. My best friend Darlene and her husband had a small reception at their house for us afterward. We left to travel back home to Atlanta, GA shortly after.

Six months later, we renewed our vows. We had a church wedding and a reception at one of the hotel ballrooms in Charleston, SC. The wedding party consisted of five bridesmaids and five groomsmen. My cousin Debra was my maid of honor. My sister-n-law Althea did the organizing and planning for the wedding in South Carolina for us. Darlene made a ten-tier wedding cake as a gift to us, and one of my cousins chauffeured us around in his limousine. We received a lot of compliments on how beautiful our wedding was.

Some time later I was facing a challenge; my monthly menstrual cycle did not come on. I really wasn't too concerned with being pregnant because of Willie's military documents that I read stating that he was sterile.

I had a slight head cold at that time and was thinking it hadn't come on because of that. That had happened once before, so I was hoping that it would have come on later that month, but it didn't. I told Willie that I felt that something was wrong. He said not to worry so much, because it may come on soon. His response provided no comfort for me. A few days later, I called my physician's office for an appointment.

That evening, after my appointment, we went out to dinner. Shortly after we began eating, Willie's stomach became upset and he vomited at the table. Five minutes after that, I began to feel nauseated. I asked the waiter to bring each of us Cokes, thinking that they would settle our stomachs.

It was just confirmation for me, as time went by, that I truly was pregnant. Willie's sickness lasted for a while, and I remember hearing people say that sometimes men may have an upset stomach when their mates are pregnant. I remembered that happening with Lee, my son's father, also.

I worried a lot that night, and I could hardly sleep. I kept asking myself how I could possibly be pregnant when I wasn't seeing any other man and knowing that Willie couldn't father any children.

A few days later, Willie went with me to the doctor. A pregnancy blood test was done and a phone number was given to me to call the lab for pre-recorded results.

Willie wanted to be with me when I called. So I waited until he got in from work. When he came into the house he asked me if I had called yet. I told him that I hadn't because I was too afraid.

When I finally gathered the nerve to call, I gave the phone to Willie so that he'd be the first to hear the news. When the call ended, he stated that the pregnancy test was positive. I passed out on the bed.

When I called to schedule another appointment, my doctor referred me to a gynecologist. Of course I was in shock with the news of being pregnant, but I was very worried about the effects of the Agent Orange causing birth defects on my unborn child. I was eager to talk with the doctor about that issue.

I was pleased to learn, that my gynecologist, Dr. Peter White, had spent time in the military and knew about Agent Orange. Willie provided him with copies of his medical records, which showed that he was sterile.

I asked Dr. White how was it possible for us to conceive given the information in Willie's file. He looked over the records and told us that over the years, Willie may have had a very low sperm count, which took this long to return to normal.

My son Lee had just returned back home from army boot camp training. I didn't know how to break the news to him. I was worried about how he would respond. Together, Willie and I ended up telling him. He was shocked, but happy that he would soon have a brother or sister.

One Saturday evening, Willie and I were out shopping. As I was trying on a jacket near a clothes rack, I felt hungry and weak all of a sudden with a sharp pain in my stomach. I dropped the jacket on the floor and walked hurriedly toward the exit door telling Willie to hurry up and come on because I needed to get something to eat quickly. All the while, Willie laughed at me saying that he never seen me move so fast. He joked about how I rushed to the car so fast like lightening had struck near me.

Every so often, Willie would bring that incident up and laugh about it because he said that it was really funny to him. It was somewhat refreshing to see this side of him in the midst of everything else.

When our baby was born, he did not make a sound. I panicked thinking that something serious had happened to him during the Cesarean birthing process. After two or three minutes, the nurses finally got him to cry. After that, they took him over to the nursing station to get him all cleaned up. Willie was a proud man to know that he fathered a son whom we had decided to name Kevon Jamar. He would affectionately call him Jamar.

On my discharge from the hospital, I was given instructions from my doctors on what I should and should not do. One of the instructions was to not walk up and down the stair steps at home for at least three weeks due to my surgery. All of the bedrooms were upstairs, so Willie would sometimes carry me up the stairs. When he did things such as this, it reminded me of the reason why I fell in love with him.

I had a lot of swelling and pain in my legs and feet after the delivery. Willie helped me out a lot around the house. One of my girlfriends, Darlene, called me a couple days after I returned home from the hospital letting me know that she was coming to stay with us for a couple of weeks to help me out. I was happy that she came because Willie's nerves were beginning to show signs of instability again. I didn't have any clue as to why this was happening.

When Darlene arrived, she took me to the doctor's office because I had excessive swelling in my legs and feet. I found out during my visit with the doctor that my blood pressure was very high and that I needed to keep my legs elevated. Dr. White wanted me back in his office in a few days. He said that if my blood pressure was still high, he was going to have me admitted back into the hospital. We left his office, picked up some lunch and stopped by one of Darlene's cousin's house that was nearby in the same area that we live. We only stayed about ten minutes. We did not get out of the car.

We arrived back at the house early that afternoon. Willie was still at the house getting ready for work. I told Darlene that I was going up stairs to talk with Willie to let him know what Dr. White said. I literally had to sit on the steps and pull myself up to the top with my arms. When I got to the bedroom door, I could tell that he was irritable. I walked past him and went straight to the bathroom to wash my hands. I didn't feel I could tell him anything at that moment.

Willie came into the bathroom and asked me why it took us so long to go to the doctor's office. I tried to explain to him what had happened but he began accusing me of seeing another man. He made me so upset to the point I just couldn't take it another second. I turned around and slapped him so hard that his eyeglasses flew off his face. I asked him how I was going to meet another man as sick as I was. Willie rushed down the stairs and left. As the evening drew into night, I started praying that he wouldn't come back home acting like a fool. I didn't want Darlene to see him like that and embarrass me.

Willie came home from work later that night. I got worried because I was so sure that he was going to act out. I was surprised when he came in the house with a pleasant look on his face asking how we were doing. Darlene had cooked dinner.

Willie fixed a plate of food and sat down at the kitchen table where we were. He laughed and talked with us the whole time. It was like nothing happened earlier that afternoon between us. He did not bring the incident up and I didn't either. It appeared to me like he had forgotten what happened. I detected shortly after I met Willie that he had a split personality problem.

Darlene took me back to the doctor a week later. I was elated to know that my blood pressure had gone down to normal range and the swelling in my legs and feet were much better.

The weekend was approaching for Darlene to return back home to her family. I thanked God for Darlene, she was a real true friend to me and fortunately by the time she left, I was able to do some things on my own. Still, Willie and Lee helped me when they were around the house.

I was on maternity leave from my job for two months. During that time, it seemed like Willie got more irritated the longer we were around each other. He continued with his outlandish accusations. One incident that really surprised me was, one day while Willie was giving Jamar a bath; he noticed a green spot on Jamar's hip. He asked me was Jamar really his baby because he never seen an African American baby with a green spot. I asked him why he'd ask a stupid question like that. He replied that only Chinese babies were born with green spots. A visit to Dr. White's office explained it all. Dr. White said that there are cases of green spots that usually seen on babies of all races and that it is caused pretty much by the baby lying more on one side in the amniotic sac surrounded by fluid. When there's a lack of circulation, it may cause discoloration.

My return to work was approaching and I needed to look for a baby sitter or a nursery for Jamar. Willie really didn't want me to go back to work. He wanted me to stay home and keep the baby because he wasn't too enthused about a nursery or a baby sitter. He was willing to work two jobs in order to keep me at home.

I told him that I was not going to give up my job and benefits just like that since I had been there for so many years. I had made up my mind to continue working just like I was doing before I met Willie and surely needed to do so since the birth of our son.

I called my supervisor at work about two weeks prior to returning to work to let her know I had not found a baby sitter or a nursery at that time. I asked for an extension to my maternity leave for a few more weeks. She told me that she didn't have a problem with the extension and she gave me a phone number to a childcare solution office. I called them up and they gave me a few childcare listings.

I called one of the numbers and spoke to the sitter, Ms. Hall. She told me that she was only allowed to have six children in her home, and she did have a space for Jamar. I went over by myself on the first visit and Ms. Hall gave me the contact information of her other parents to call and get references if I wanted. I did call a couple of parents and was very impressed from what they told me about Ms. Hall. I told Willie all about her and he visited Ms. Hall with me a couple days later. Willie was impressed with her as well. Everything worked out perfectly. But on the first day, I dropped Jamar off and arrived at work an hour late because I didn't want to leave him. When I did get to work, I cried and called Ms. Hall all day long until she told me not to worry myself because Jamar would be fine.

After Jamar got a little older, he got so attached to Ms. Hall that he would be crying and fighting to stay with her when I would come to get him.

Chapter 3

Willie had gotten to the place where he just wanted to be so protective and guard us in everything that we did. It was like he was paranoid of everything. It seemed as though he didn't want me out of his sight. Before I met him, I was very outgoing. He didn't have any trust in me. The false accusations were really hard to handle.

Willie got to the point where he didn't want to do anything but stay at home and find every little thing to fuss at me about. He confronted me about Lee coming in after midnight, especially on the weekend. I tried to explain to him that Lee sometimes didn't get off from his job until after 11:00 p.m. After that, he and his friends would go out. Willie told me that he didn't care what I said, all he wanted me to do was to tell Lee to be in the house by midnight in order to respect our home or he could just spend the night out with his friends. That was a battle for a while. Lee was always a humble young man. Even though Willie used to fuss all the time, Lee never disrespected him. Lee never even talked back to Willie or me. When I saw Willie getting ready to start an argument, I would just walk away so he wouldn't fuss so much. I truly didn't want Lee to see us arguing.

Eventually Willie extended Lee's curfew to 1:00 A.M. The only reason he did was because I would ask Lee to baby sit Jamar sometimes so that Willie and I could go out. I made Willie feel guilty, because when we went out, we sometimes got back after midnight and I didn't think that was fair to Lee.

Lee would do anything for Willie but Willie seemed like he couldn't bond with Lee. I believe that Willie was a little jealous of Lee because of Lee's and my relationship.

One Friday evening, Lee got off work around 6:00 p.m. he had plans to go out later that night. Willie was at work. I asked Lee to keep Jamar so I could go to the grocery store before he left the house. While I was gone, Willie called and asked to speak to me. Lee told him where I had gone. Willie called back an hour later and I answered the phone. He asked me where I was when he called earlier. I told him that I went to the store. He told me to stop lying to him and when he got to the house, I needed to have a better answer than that. I hung up the phone in his face and just asked God to not let him come home with that foolishness.

I was so relieved that Lee had left the house before Willie came. When Willie came in, I had all the store items on the table to prove to him that I was telling the truth. He still didn't believe me. He started accusing me of doing everything under the sun. I told him to please stop it because I was really fed up with the accusations and he was just acting like a crazy man. When I said that, he really snapped and grabbed me by my hair and told me he didn't like me calling him names. I fought him to make him turn loose my hair. We started tussling and I scratched him in his chest with my fingernails. He bled a little. I got away from him and I ran upstairs to call the police. He knew what I was going to do, so he ran right behind me.

When I picked up the phone to call, I did manage to dial 911, but I couldn't talk because he knocked the phone out of my hand. The phone was hanging off the hook as we were tussling. A few minutes later, the police came knocking on the door around mid-night. Willie told me since I called them, then I must go open the door.

The police talked with us and then asked Willie to step outside with him so they could talk alone. The policeman told Willie that it would be best for him to leave the house. Willie put a few personal items in an overnight bag and left.

Willie called me around 1:00 A.M. I answered and he told me that he was sorry and that he needed to come back to the house and go to bed. I told him no and hung the phone up.

Shortly after that, Lee came home. Five minutes later, we heard someone knocking at the front door. Lee said that it was Willie. He opened the door for him. I didn't tell Lee anything about what happened prior to Willie coming back to the house. I was really hoping and praying that he wouldn't say anything to me. Willie went into the family room and locked the door. I was so happy that he didn't start up again. About an hour later, I heard him snoring. I just thanked God for that.

The next morning, I got up and went downstairs to prepare breakfast. Shortly after I finished, Willie came downstairs to eat with us. He did not bring up anything that happened the night before. I told God that it seemed to me

38

like Willie really didn't understand his actions. One day he would act like a perfect gentleman and the next day, it was like a tornado hit.

Willie didn't have any flare-ups for about a week. I was surprised when he asked me to call Annie and see if she was going out and if so, I could join her. He knew Annie and I loved dancing. He told me that he would baby sit Jamar. I was shocked. I acted on that right away. I called Annie and we decided to go to the club. She picked me up around 10:00 P.M. We danced, ate and had a great time. I guessed Willie felt that I needed a little break. And I did.

I informed Annie that I'd like to leave the club at 12:30 A.M. She said that the dance floor didn't get heated up until midnight. We ended up leaving at 1:00 A.M. Annie dropped me off at my house close to 1:30 A.M. As I walked toward the stairs, I saw Willie sitting at the top of the staircase. I asked him what was wrong. He said he was sitting there waiting to see how long it would be before I got home. He asked me if I knew what time it was. I told him yes and I started justifying everything we did. He didn't want to hear it. At that point he started accusing me of having met someone else and not being where I told him we were. I even tried showing him the stamp the club assistant placed on my hand. He told me that that didn't mean anything. I asked him to call Annie and ask her.

I asked Willie why he volunteered to let me go out and then turn around and harass me with accusations afterwards. He told me to get my stinking self to the bathroom and clean myself because he felt like killing me. I detected alcohol on his breath. When he made that

statement, I did not say anything else to him. I quickly got
out of his way and went to my bedroom and sat on the end
of the bed in tears, pleading and asking God not to let
Willie hurt me. Although he had fallen off to sleep
downstairs in the recliner, I was afraid to close my eyes to
get some sleep. I stayed awake until the early morning.
After that episode, I kept my eyes on him constantly.

The next day, Willie was a totally different person. I
just couldn't figure him out. I began to think that something
was seriously wrong with him, but I had no idea what it
was. I started praying and asking God to please show me
what was wrong with Willie.

Through all of what he was putting me through, I still
couldn't get mad and seek revenge on him because my
heart wouldn't allow me to do that. He would upset me a
lot when he went into his raging mode. But when I saw him
doing a little better, I would try my best to keep him happy
and calm finding all kinds of things to do and I would go
overboard in planning places to go hoping that make things
better.

Willie gradually became secluded from the family.
He would be in another part of the house by himself. I
would ask what was wrong and he would snap at me and
tell me not to ask him any questions. I started thinking he
was upset with me about something. Willie started
distancing himself from the people he used to be around
before he met me. He didn't like talking on the phone much
either. He became withdrawn. Sometimes it seemed like he
would sit and study over what he was going to fuss with me
about. I began doing some studying of my own, trying to
see what made him upset so quickly.

One of the things I learned was that if I ever wanted to polish my finger and toe nails, I'd have to do it without him seeing me doing it because he would always ask me who I was trying to impress or going to see. It was pretty strange that he did not question me if I had it on already and he did not see me putting it on.

I finally realized that I was falling under Willie's controllable power. He didn't allow me to do much of anything away from the home and hardly anything inside our home. He wanted to make sure he kept up with every movement I made. For example, he'd be downstairs and I'd be upstairs or vice versa. Very soon, he would come to where I was to see what I was doing.

One day, I left Jamar with Willie to go to the pharmacy to get some cold medicine. Jamar was sick. I was gone for about forty-five minutes. As soon as I came home, Willie accused me of being somewhere I shouldn't be. Of course, when I tried to defend myself, he told me that he didn't want to hear my lies. At this point, I just threw up my hands and said whatever.

Willie continued with his cycle of accusations each time I left him alone with Jamar. After that, I started taking Jamar with me practically everywhere I went. I did that because I was trying to see if Willie would slack up on the accusations against me. After I started taking Jamar with me, I detected that Willie was not accusing me as much as he did before I started taking Jamar with me. I could leave with Jamar during the mornings and not return until late in the evening. As long as I brought something back to eat for Willie, he was okay. Sometimes when we got back, Willie would be gone out somewhere. I was glad when I saw that

41

his car wasn't in the garage or parked out side. That always meant that I didn't have to argue.

Willie could be gone all day long, have a pocket full of money and would not stop to buy himself food to eat. He would come back home hungry and head straight to the kitchen to see if I had cooked. I knew how he was, so I would always have food prepared for him. I would ask him sometimes, why he would not stop and get himself something to eat when he was out? He said that I needed to stop asking him dumb questions.

One weekend, Willie accepted an invitation for us to attend a function in Alabama being given by a friend of his. I was not able to go with him. Willie left that Friday morning and came back Sunday evening.

After he got settled in, I asked him about the trip. The conversation went well as he shared the events of his trip. I was so elated that he enjoyed himself. I was hoping that he would go away often and do things that he liked doing. I wanted him to be more at peace with himself and us.

One night while Willie was downstairs and I was upstairs changing Jamar's diaper, the phone rang. It was my cousin Ruthie. She'd called to check on us. After about five minutes, I heard Willie coming up the stairs. When he came into the room, he had a mean look on his face. I was sitting at the end of the bed holding Jamar and talking with Ruthie. All of a sudden Willie asked me if being on the phone was all I had to do. I covered the phone with my hand and told him that it was Ruthie. He told me that he did not care who it was. I asked him why he always had a problem with me talking on the phone. He said the reason was that I gossiped too much. I just shook my head because that was not so. It wasn't like I could talk to him because he wasn't a good communicator. I ended my call with Ruthie very quickly. When I hung the phone up, I told him that it was really sad that I couldn't talk on the phone without him having something to say against it. I further asserted to him, that I could hardly go to the bathroom unless he was on my heels.

It became apparent that Willie had a problem with everything that I did. To save an argument, I would return calls whenever he left the house. When I heard the garage door going up, I'd hurry and get off the phone. It was like he didn't want to miss out on anything I did.

One Saturday night we had another blow out argument. He snapped at me and got so angry that he bald up one of his fists as if he was going to hit me. I was really afraid. The next day he was all happy go lucky, like nothing had ever happened.

It seemed like Willie was fighting something deep within himself that seemed to be difficult to release. He wouldn't open up much to tell me anything. He really didn't spend much quality time with us because he was often irritated. I would pray and ask God to please forgive me for not discerning whether He wanted me to get out of this unhealthy relationship. I also asked God to please show me what to do.

I remembered praying that I wanted a Godly man who would love me. I wanted for us to have one or two children. God answered my prayer. He gave me Jamar. I knew Willie loved us unconditionally, but it was so difficult for him to show his emotions.

One of the greatest things that I admired about Willie was that he studied and meditated on the Word of God. When I first met Willie, I attended church with him often. I really did enjoy the services.

Lee and a friend of his had just started attending another local church. Lee came home one Sunday evening and told us that we should go and check out the services there because it was much closer to our home. The next Sunday, Willie and I went with Lee, and were very impressed with the Bishop's sermon. After that Sunday, we continued worshipping there and ended up joining the church.

While some of my relatives were in town for the weekend, they stopped by the house that Friday evening for a visit. Willie was at work. I took them out on a spur of the moment and showed them around Atlanta. Willie called the house several times and got worried because no one answered the phone. I did not call him at work to tell him that we were leaving the house. However, he knew that my family was going to stop by.

Willie yelled at me that night about not respecting him enough to call and let him know that we were going out. I told him that I didn't think it was going to be a problem. Willie told me that I must've had an arrangement with my family to drop me off at my man's house. I responded that another man was the farthest thing from my mind and that I wasn't looking to find one.

My relatives stopped back by our house before they traveled back home. His conversation with them was very polite. That was a relief because I was certain he was going to embarrass me.

A couple days later, he brought the incident up again saying that I didn't have to go sneaking around on him. I told him he could think whatever he wanted to. That statement really upset him. He became enraged and started kicking whatever was near him. I prayed that God would help Willie to see the truth.   Willie kept fussing and kicking things around to the point that I became afraid of him.

Chapter 4

A few days later, Willie started his mess again. The reason this time was because one of my co-workers was celebrating her birthday and invited me to come that Friday evening to a restaurant. She wanted everyone to meet at 7:00 p.m. I mentioned it to Willie a few days before and told him that I was going to try and go. He asked me what I was going to do with Jamar since he would be at work. I told him that Lee was going to baby sit.

Willie called the house around 9:30 p.m. and realized I hadn't made it home. I returned shortly after ten o'clock and Willie called again. The first thing he wanted to know was where I had been for three hours. I tried justifying again, but he didn't let me.

When Willie got home, he began arguing with me, telling me that I didn't give him an answer. I tried telling him that he should factor in the time it takes to get to a place and the time it takes to get the food. He didn't want to hear any of that; he just called me a liar.

Lee was home and heard us arguing. He pulled me to the side when Willie went into another room and asked why we were arguing. I told him why and Lee just shook his head and sighed. I knew Lee wanted to intervene, but I told him not to.

I detected that Willie wasn't aware of his behavior. Whenever he was in a good mood, I would feel comfortable asking Willie why he acted the way he did toward me. He ended up accusing me of making him look like the bad guy. He didn't even remember the things he did or said the majority of times.

I just kept on praying for God to change Willie and make him a better person with a new attitude. Nothing I said or did was getting through to Willie and my prayers weren't being answered.

Two of my cousins from South Carolina came down to stay with us for the weekend. That Saturday evening they planned to go out to the mall and a restaurant. They asked me if I wanted to go with them. I told them that I needed to check to see if Willie would keep Jamar.

My cousins were down the hall when they heard me ask Willie. He blurted out to me that he wasn't a babysitter. Then he started to show out again. I was so embarrassed.

I walked out of the room and told my cousins that they should leave without me. I tried covering the incident with a lie, telling them that Willie was upset about something else and got more irritated when I asked him to keep Jamar. I told them to please overlook what they heard and that Willie didn't mean what he said.

When my cousins left out the door, Willie yelled down the staircase that I could go and that I should be back at a decent time. I took no time telling my cousins to wait for me.

We went to the mall and then to a restaurant. When we came out of the restaurant to leave, my cousin discovered she had locked her keys in the car. My heart fluttered. I thought to myself that this was all I needed. I didn't want to call Willie because I knew he'd think I was lying. I called him anyway because I knew that roadside assistance wouldn't get to us for another hour or two.

Willie wasn't to please about what I had to say, but he ended up coming to where we were to see if he could help so we wouldn't have to wait so long for roadside assistance.

When he got there, he tried, but didn't have any luck in unlocking the door with the hanger. He stayed there with us until roadside assistance came. I was very happy that he did come so he could see that I was telling the truth. When we got back home, Willie got Jamar ready for bed. After that, he went into another room and locked himself inside. He did not say anything to us the rest of the night.

Willie and I were dining at a restaurant one evening. As we waited for our orders, I asked him if he had ever killed or harmed anyone during his tour at Nam. He looked at me coldly and told me never to ask that question again. The bitter sincerity in his voice made me worry. At that point, I just assumed that he did kill people, (the enemies and the innocent) being at war on the battlefield in Vietnam in order to stay alive.

One night as we were watching television, I flipped through the channels trying to find a good movie. I stopped on a channel that had an old war movie playing. Willie saw it briefly and told me to hurry up and change the channel. I asked him why he didn't want to watch it. He told me that

48

he did not like watching war movies because they would only bring back haunting memories from the war.

One Saturday night, we were lying in bed with Jamar in between us. We'd fallen asleep watching a movie. Lee was out of town. All of a sudden Willie sat up in the bed and was yelling at someone telling them to get out of the bedroom and to leave him alone before he killed them. I asked Willie what was wrong with him and to whom was he talking? He then told me that he was talking to two black men dressed in black clothing with long black hair and red eyes standing at the foot of the bed. He became outrageous even to the point of going toward the bedroom windows, pointing his finger at them telling them to get out right now and don't come back. I assumed that they were evil spirits of the enemies from Vietnam that he may have killed, demons or ghosts that were haunting him.

Willie told me to look toward the windows and see them leaving. I told him that I didn't see anyone and I asked what was wrong. He regained composure and said that he had had a real bad nightmare. It frightened me so badly that I told Willie, nightmare or not, I was getting out of that bedroom. I took Jamar, went into the other bedroom and laid down. Willie came to the room and told me to come back to bed and that he was very sorry that had happened. I told him I was too afraid to go back. Willie kept apologizing to me and told me that the next time something like that happened, he'd try and keep it to himself.

Willie was often up throughout the night. I could hardly sleep because of that. Some nights he would grit his teeth or wake up drenched with sweat. Other nights he would wake up shaking as if he were having seizures.

Jamar's crib was in our room near the windows. Jamar cried sometimes all night long. I couldn't figure out why he wouldn't sleep. I started to wonder if the same things that haunted Willie were haunting Jamar. I prayed to God to protect my family. As Jamar got older, he cried more and more in the crib. I realized that he was afraid to sleep alone. We let him sleep with us for quite some time. Willie tried very hard not to tell me what was going on with him, because I believed that he was afraid he'd risk losing us.

A few weeks later, we went to Charleston, SC for my class reunion. We had a wonderful time. He met some of my classmates who were in the military that had flown in from overseas. Surprisingly, Willie related well to them.

The next Saturday night while I was sleeping, I heard someone crying. It wasn't Jamar because he was lying next to me. Lee was in his room and Willie was in the guest room. I got up and went to see who was crying. I went to Willie first and I discovered him balled up in a corner crying. My heart got weak. I didn't know what to do but ask what was wrong. He told me that he couldn't tell me and that he knew I didn't want to know. All I could do was comfort him by massaging him and telling him that everything would be all right. I went to get him a snack and stayed in the room with him all night.

Willie slept for a few hours. We had planned on going to church that Sunday morning. When he woke up, he told me that he wasn't going to church. I was so exhausted and didn't feel like going either. Willie thought I was going, but I left the guest room and got into my bed. The alarm was going to go off in a couple of hours; I turned it off before it did. Willie came down to the room later on that morning to see why I was not up getting ready to go to church. I told him that I was really tired and was not going.

Willie seemed to have had an amnesia attack or something when I told him that I was not going. He didn't understand why I wasn't going. He started fussing and telling me that I was lazy and that being tired wasn't an excuse for not going to church. I tried to remind him about what had happened the night before, but he didn't want to hear it. I told him to get out of the room and to leave me alone. He then slammed the door behind him as he was leaving.

Feeling guilty about not going to church, I reluctantly got up. I sat on the bed a little while before getting dressed and thought of what had just happened. I finally got Jamar and myself ready for church, prepared a little breakfast and went on to the 11:00 am service. I cried the whole way to church.

I was glad that I'd gone to church because the sermon was beautiful. I prayed fervently for God to heal Willie's mind in every way and to rid Willie of whatever it was that was bothering him. After service, I stopped by the grocery store to pick up a few items and came home. I got home around 3:00 p.m. When I walked in the door, Willie started up again by telling me that he knew I wasn't at church all that time. I told him that I was stuck in the church traffic for nearly an hour after leaving and stopped off to the grocery store to pick up a few items. He saw those bags that I brought in. I was upset because he knew exactly how congested our church traffic was. His fussing led to his questioning me as to what was the message the Bishop preached about. This time, I just let him fuss. I just ignored it, got Jamar situated, and started to prepare dinner. Later on that evening, Willie's attitude changed. He was in a better mood.

When Willie had his episodes, I would sometimes criticize him for acting like a child. He'd get upset with me when I said that. A few nights later, he fell asleep lying across the foot of the bed.

As he was sleeping, he started shaking as if he was having a seizure or something, night sweats and even talking to people in his sleep telling them not to kill him. I nudged him with my foot. When he woke up, I asked him about it. He apologized again and went into the guest bedroom.

I didn't know what to do to help him. Even the medications that he was on didn't seem to help much with his relaxation and sleep. I made sure he took all of his meds. Deep down I knew that there was something going on inside of him and the medications weren't helping the way I thought it would.

One evening, Willie called me at work. He told me that he had gotten off work early. I detected something was wrong by his voice. We decided to discuss things further when I got home. I started to worry thinking that I might've done something wrong. I left worked, picked up Jamar, and prayed all the way home.

When I got home, I was relieved to find out that his news wasn't about me but about people at work who he'd said were lying on him about something. He never told me the entire incident. The only other thing he said was that his

52

colleagues were messing with the wrong person when they messed with him.

I told him when he goes back to work the next day, just try and overlook what people say or what he may hear. I told him that he must not take everything to heart and to do his job the best he could. He went back to work the next day and he told me everything went fine.

A couple nights later, I had dinner prepared for him. I would always sit with him when he came in to eat. He told me that he would like for me to try to stay up long enough for him to talk with me about something pertaining to him.

Willie finally broke down that night and shared with me that he felt that something was seriously wrong with him. He said he believed the problem was going on ever since he came back from Vietnam. He went on to say that few of his family members and friends detected that he was acting differently.

When I met Willie, he was seeing a primary care physician, Dr. Jones at the VA. He also was seeing a private practice primary care physician, Dr. Crawford. One night as we were talking, Willie all of a sudden asked me if I would do him a big favor by going to the VA hospital with him. I asked him why he needed me to go with him. He said because we needed to talk with the physician about the outburst behaviors, the nightmares, and everything else that I was experiencing with him. I was hesitant because I did not know where to start. I asked Willie if other people in his life that were very close to him had experienced some of the things that I experienced with him. He told me yes, they had, but they called him a delirious fool. When he asked them to go with him to seek help, he felt that they were ashamed of him and would not go. After he told me that, he asked me to keep a diary of what occurred so I wouldn't forget anything when we saw the physician. My prayers were answered. God had revealed the truth to Willie.

Willie introduced me to Dr. Jones. At the end of the session, Dr. Jones asked Willie if he ever been tested for or diagnosed with PTSD (post traumatic stress disorder). Willie told her that he hadn't. Dr. Jones told us that Willie showed signs of PTSD and he needed an immediate psychological evaluation. We asked her what was PTSD. Dr. Jones said that PTSD is a mental disorder that Willie may have due to the trauma of combat and he need to be treated for it. Dr. Jones said if not treated; it can cause extreme affect on Willie and his family, adding that some of his symptoms may never go away. Dr. Jones also mentioned that the name PTSD came about around 1980, which replaced the previous name called "shell shock" (fatigue) which many soldiers were being treated for at that time.

On our way home, Willie expressed that he got irritated with Dr. Jones because he felt like he was being stigmatized and made to feel as though he were crazy. I tried to encourage him so that he wouldn't feel that way. My efforts were of little effect because he ranted during our entire drive home. At one point, he blamed me for informing Dr. Jones of his past behavior.

When we arrived home, I went into the kitchen to prepare dinner. I was washing a skillet when Willie came into the kitchen area and called me a stupid fool. My anger led me to yell back at him suggesting that he find someone else to go with him to his next appointment because he didn't seem to appreciate me. Only God knew how difficult it was dealing with Willie.

A couple of days later, late one evening, I got a call from one of Willie's supervisors telling me that I needed to come to his work place right away. I thought he had taken sick or got hurt. Willie had asked his supervisor to call me. I was so nervous and worried about what could possibly be wrong. When I got there, I was relieved when I saw Willie sitting in the office. Willie had an intense argument with one of his supervisors and took his anger out on one of his co-workers by picking up an iron pipe to strike him. I was relieved to learn that he didn't hit the man.

Because of Willie's job performance, and the isolation of similar events, the company decided not to call the police or press any charges. They suspended him and told him that he needed to seek medical attention immediately for his outrageous behavior. I asked Willie if he had any previous incidents at his workplace. He said that he had but they weren't as bad as that incident.

A few days later, I went with him to his scheduled psychiatric evaluation with Dr. Knight. The test results determined that Willie indeed was suffering from PTSD along with depression, which often accompanies the disorder. She told us that there is no cure for PTSD, but it could only be managed with treatments. She stated that PTSD could affect all areas of one's life and it is usually brought on by some kinds of trauma, which can cause nightmares, flashbacks, anxiety attacks, and more.

Dr. Knight said that depression is also a mental illness and some of the symptoms are suicidal thoughts, irritability, stress and poor memory. Dr. Knight said, soldiers on the battlefield normally have to make instant life and death decisions.

Dr. Knight told Willie that she could help him only if he was willing to accept it. She told him the first step was to have him admitted in the VA hospital for four to six weeks. She said they would start a regimen treatment for PTSD, which included different medications and psychotherapy. When Dr. Knight said that, Willie got so upset. He said that she might as well call him crazy and didn't want to be in a psychiatric ward.

Dr. Knight was calm because she had seen so many patients with PTSD. She stepped out of the office to allow us privacy to make a decision. I tried to convince him to go through the program. He accused me of wanting him out the house so that I could be with another man. I prayed to God to change Willie's mind. While we waited for Dr. Knight, I continued to encourage him to get the help she was offering to him. I knew that Willie was indeed suffering and struggling with the symptoms of PTSD and depression that Dr. Knight mentioned to us.

A few days later and after much convincing from Dr. Knight, myself, and an old Vietnam comrade of Willie's who had called and told him about his success with PTSD. Willie decided to get admitted into the hospital. I was so relieved when he said that he wanted to get help.

The day that I was taking him to the hospital to be admitted, I had everything he needed packed in his suitcase except his Bible. When he discovered that he did not have it, he made me go back home right then to get it. Willie loved reading the Word.   That was one of the qualities I admired most about him.

Dr. Knight had requested documents about the incident that took place at Willie's job. Willie's employer had been notified that he would be in the treatment program. Willie eventually confessed his feelings and emotions behind his actions. At that moment, I started feeling closer to him. I understood him better and I wanted to protect him as if he were a child.

Willie was very irritable while adjusting to the hospital and the medications. I went to visit him as my scheduled allowed.

Normally, I visited Willie before picking Jamar up from the babysitter. But one evening, I worked late, and had to pick Jamar up first. When I arrived, the medical assistant went to get Willie. When Willie came into the lobby, he was agitated. I asked him what was wrong. He asked me why was I late. Of course I tried telling him what happened, but he wasn't hearing me. And of course he accused me of stopping off somewhere else. I was hurt and said that I was trying to do the best I could.

I hastily walked out the hospital and looked back and saw Willie coming toward us. I got inside the car and turned the ignition on and was slowly driving away. Willie was fussing and walking along side the car. I let down the driver's side window and asked him to go back inside the hospital. Suddenly, he grabbed my hair and was pulling it. I stopped the car, as I tussled to break free of his grip. Finally, I knocked his hand out of my hair and sped away.

I cried all the way home. I prayed that God would allow the treatments to work for Willie. I didn't go back the next day because I didn't know what to expect. The following day he called and asked me to bring a couple items he needed from the store. When I arrived, I was waiting for him to start up about the parking lot incident but he never mentioned it. He acted as if it never happened. He was very calm and pleasant. He even told me to be careful going home and to kiss Jamar for him. He was so concerned. I left the hospital thanking the Lord. I felt sorry for Willie. I hated seeing him in his disheveled state of mind. I wished he'd sought treatment early on in his illness.

Each week at the hospital, Willie became a little better. In his last week at the hospital, Dr. Knight went over his discharge plan.   She stressed that he had to take his medication as prescribed and noted him as disabled due to PTSD. She also set him up with anger management classes. I was truly impressed with Dr. Knight, her professionalism, and her knowledge of PTSD. We left the hospital knowing that even though Willie went through treatment, the doctor said it could take months or years to control PTSD. Dr. Knight told us that PTSD could be a problem that Willie may have for the rest of his life.

Willie was doing okay handling his PTSD, especially when he took his meds the proper way. He'd have a flare up occasionally, but he really got in a heap whenever he walked through the doors of the VA hospital. He'd get agitated and blow up at anybody, even me if I opened my mouth. There were other veterans in the hospitals that I witnessed acting pretty much like Willie.

Willie was doing well after the first treatment and wanted to visit his family more often. He and his cousin

Patsy were very close. When we visited her, she'd always tell him that he'd better treat me right or she'd chew him out. I started to tell her how bad he treated me sometimes, but I didn't because I knew that he was suffering from PTSD that caused him not to be himself sometimes. I came to realize that his actions were not intentional.

Willie received a letter from the VA hospital that the eight-week PTSD program was about to start again. Willie was adamant about not attending; it had been a year since his first stay. He got upset about me coaxing him to go and I asked why he was so angry. He said that he didn't want to go because he thought they might try to kill him. He told me to call and tell them that he wouldn't be attending. I called Dr. Knight and told her. She asked why he didn't want to go. I told her that he had a problem with that location. And said he just did not like being there. I didn't tell her anything about what he said about them killing him. Dr. Knight then mentioned to me that they had another program like that located in Augusta, GA. I told Willie about it and surprisingly he agreed to go two hours away to stay for the next eight weeks.

Approximately three weeks later, Willie was admitted in the VA hospital in Augusta, GA. I was elated to know that three of his friends were there also in the program. I went to visit Willie once during the week and on weekends. I also attended the programs that were open to family members. I became acquainted with some other veteran's wives. The VA had a program that was a specially designed program that offered great understanding of the impact of PTSD. It involved helping family members understanding the disorder and provided skills in managing emotions. We spent weeks attending the class.   I learned a lot about PTSD.

Things were up and down with Willie and I as we struggled through his varying emotions.   We would soon face a family tragedy, when his close cousin Patsy had fallen ill. We went to see her and were hurt over her illness. We were going through so much at that time.

A week later, we received a call notifying us that Patsy had died. After attending the funeral, Willie decided that we needed a little vacation.   We went up to the Tennessee Mountains.

After we returned back home, Willie got very depressed over the loss of Patsy and stopped taking his mediations. He said that he was tired of everything. I knew once he stopped taking his medications, he would be unable to control his emotions.   I pleaded for him to continue taking his medicine. He refused my pleas.

When Willie stopped taking his pills, it was one thing when he yelled at me, but he started yelling at Jamar who was a toddler. I tried again desperately to convince him to take his medications. He became more rowdy and belligerent. He started to complain more about pain in his back and legs. When he was frustrated, he'd take it all out on me. He made it seem like I was responsible for his pain. Two weeks later, Willie started back taking his medications.

.

Chapter 5

Valentine's Day was always special for Willie and I. When I came into the house, he was sitting at the kitchen table. I presented him with the candy and roses. To my surprise, he looked at me and asked why I bought the items. I said it was Valentine's Day. I thought he was just kidding about not knowing what day it was. He said that he was going out and that he'd be right back. I went up stairs looking for a present that he might've stashed away. When I didn't find anything, I knew he really didn't know that it was Valentine's Day. I prayed that it was the usual male slip of losing track of special days.

Willie came back a couple of hours later. He surprised me with a dinner from Red Lobster and a Valentine's basket filled with goodies. He gave me a hug and a kiss. I was thankful and prayed that the Lord would help him to remember celebratory days because it meant a lot to me.   Willie's birthday was a few weeks later. He didn't even know it was his birthday until I came home with a Baskin Robin's ice cream cake and dinner. He was sitting on the couch watching TV. I went to the kitchen and placed the candles in the cake. When he came into the kitchen, Jamar and I began singing Happy Birthday. He looked at me in bewilderment, but I could tell that he was grateful.

For Mother's day, Willie and I went to his mother's burial site to place some flowers on her grave. On our way back home, I asked him to take me out to dinner. He said that I wasn't his mother and that he was not in the mood to stop anywhere. I was not angry with him; I figured he was rather emotional after coming from his mother's grave.

Father's day came and I treated Willie to brunch and a comedy show. Later that night, we dinned in N.W. Atlanta where there was a jazz band. Willie enjoyed himself. I loved it when my husband was happy.

I made the decision to start school to become a medical assistant after leaving my full time job because caring for people makes me happy. I was blessed to have landed a part-time job at an after school program shortly thereafter. It was convenient for me; I'd taken Jamar out of the private day care and placed him in the program where I worked. My new job was good about working around my school schedule. I was able to study and complete some of my homework while the children were eating their snacks and napping.

One day, one of the teachers confronted me about Jamar's erratic behavior. She'd told me that Jamar jumped on another student and started beating him. She had to literally pull him off the student. I was shocked at the news. The teacher shared what had happen with the other child's mother. I sat down and talked with her as well. I thought this might've been an isolated incident and that it wouldn't happen again. I asked the teacher to put him on strict punishment whenever he misbehaves.

Jamar continued to have difficulties not wanting to sleep alone. He never went to bed on his own. I had to lie in bed with him until he fell asleep. Jamar made it a habit to come into our bedroom in the early morning hours and sleep in between us. Willie got irritated with Jamar's behavior and made him go back to his room. Jamar cried but that didn't stop Willie from making him sleep in his own bed. Jamar started sneaking into our room to my bedside, and nudged me to move over. Eventually Willie found out that he was doing that and yelled at him.   Jamar continued this pattern for several years.   Jamar's behavior made me wonder if they were a result of seeing Willie's erratic behavior.

The time came for Willie to go back to the VA hospital for the six to eight week treatment programs. I could tell that Jamar missed Willie because during one of our visits to see his dad, Jamar cried uncontrollably when he realized that he wouldn't be going back home with us. Willie talked with Jamar and calmed him down by telling him that he would be home soon. The next weekend I went to see Willie; I left Jamar with my cousin Debra so that he would not fret. Willie had become a little emotional about Jamar's feelings.

Willie finally had surgery on his back due to a herniated disk. During this time, it seemed like he took all of his pain and frustration out on Jamar and me. I hung in there, even scheduled my schoolwork and part-time job around taking care of him. To cheer Willie up, I planned a surprise birthday party for him. He enjoyed it, or so I thought. When the party was over, Willie stormed after me asking me why I even bothered to throw him a party and knowing that he probably wasn't up for having many people around. I told him that I was trying to do something nice for him and I thought it would be great for him to stay home since he recently had surgery. He walked away and mumbled, what was so great about it?

Months later, it was time for another set of treatments. This time, he made sure that the staff scheduled him to be discharged during the week of my graduation so he would be there. He also told the staff that he had invested too much into my education and that he wouldn't miss it for the world and if they made him miss it, he would turn the VA hospital upside down. After my graduation ceremony, some of our family and friends came by the house to take a part in my graduation celebration. Willie told them how proud he was of me. He also stated that he was glad to have his wife's undivided attention again. He was so elated.

One evening Willie went to the store and was involved in an accident. Willie was very upset. When he got home, he told me what happened and that I should call the police. I looked at the car and told him that there was no need to call the police because there was nothing wrong with the car other than a little scratch on the front end bumper, not enough to get a police involve. Willie started to fuss at Jamar and me. Jamar asked his dad why was he mad at him, then started crying. Willie got really upset and was going after Jamar with his belt to whip him. He told me not to try to stop him or he would whip me too. I took Jamar upstairs out of his dad's way to avoid the whipping. Fortunately, Willie did not come upstairs behind us.

Willie was due for psychological evaluation a few days later. I went to the VA hospital prior to his visit and delivered two letters to the two doctors that were to evaluate him. The letters stated that Jamar and I were becoming more afraid of Willie and his behavior. In my letter I asked the doctors to do what ever it took to make my husband a better person. The hospital sent transportation for Willie that day. I did not get to go with him.

On a later visit, I was told that Willie really acted out when he was there for his evaluation. He ranted and raved about how people were constantly trying to put him down. He even threatened to bring a gun and ransack the hospital. Willie stated that he was taking someone else down with him. The doctor immediately sent him back home; he didn't get to see the second doctor. A few weeks later Willie received his test results stating that he was suffering from severe PTSD. At that time, there was a major change in his medications.

Meanwhile, Jamar's behavior in school was nothing to celebrate. It seemed like I was at his school trying to correct his serious behavioral problems more than I was at work. After discussing the matter several times with his pediatrician, she suggested having him checked by a child psychologist. I told her about Willie's behavior. She shared this was a great factor in Jamar's behavior. She further suggested that Willie keep his conduct in check because Jamar could easily pick up on some of the learned behaviors. I took Jamar to the psychologist a few times, but it didn't change his thoughts. I just continued to work with his Pre-K and kindergarten teachers at the time on different ways that we could help him. Jamar would throw temper tantrums at times when he didn't have his way, wouldn't keep still, had difficulty sitting down quietly, and not listening at times. He also had a very short attention span. However, the teachers found him to be bright, intelligent, creative and smart.

Jamar's behavior would get the best of Willie. He'd get a dose of his own medicine each time he'd encountered Jamar. One time, on our way to visit relatives, Willie turned the car around and drove us back home because Jamar was so out of control. I started slacking up on taking Jamar to the psychologist until eventually I stopped all together. I was tired of running back and forth when nothing seemed to be working. Willie did not offer too much support.

I was thankful for a trip that we'd taken to one of Willie's aunts. She was able to witness how Willie was roughly disciplining Jamar. She told Willie to leave him alone and that he better not touch him while we were in her house. Of course, that didn't sit too well with Willie, but he sure didn't touch Jamar for the remainder of our stay.

Willie was strongly addicted to cigarettes. I believed that he used them to cope with his problems. I always got on him about how second hand smoke could cause asthma in small children. I often turned the TV channel on anti-cigarettes commercials and specials so that Willie could see it for himself health problems that could be brought on to one's body by smoking. Sometimes after Willie finish looking at the information on TV; he would pick up his car keys and head to the corner store to purchase more cigarettes. Many times Jamar ask his father to quit smoking cigarettes because he did not want him to die. Willie would tell Jamar that he was going to quit. I started complaining to Willie not to smoke in the house and suggested he go outside to smoke. That did not set to well with him. He stormed that if he couldn't smoke in his home, there was no need for him to be living in it. I kept on nagging him about it until he gave up smoking at least inside the house.

Jamar's school administrator called Willie to tell him that he needed to pick Jamar up because of his disruptive behavior. Willie called me and told me that the teacher said Jamar was throwing pencils at students and talking out of turn. He gave me a decision to make if he had to go get Jamar, it would mean trouble for him or I could pick him up. I told him that I would pick Jamar up because he probably would spank him right in front of the class, and then I would have to be the one to bail him out of jail. I called the teacher and told her to call me not Willie whenever Jamar acted out.

Jamar's fear of his father got so bad that when he heard me pick up my keys to go somewhere, he would run out the door ahead of me to get in the car. Jamar didn't care if he was partially clothed, he just didn't want to stay with his father.

I decided to plan a vacation to spend quality time with my family and friends. I asked Willie a few weeks prior if he'd like to go and he said he didn't want to. I was so happy because I knew that I'd have a peaceful trip.

The Thursday before my departure that Saturday, I started cooking enough food for him to last the duration of my stay. All he had to do was to warm it up. I asked Willie again out of courtesy that Friday, if he was sure he didn't want to go, hoping that he would still say no. To my surprise, he told me that he'd go. I almost hit the floor: So much for a peaceful vacation.

Willie wanted to drive his car. I figured this was a control issue. On our way there one of my cousins called me on my cell phone to ask if we wanted to go to a birthday party. I asked Willie if he wanted to go. He said no. I asked him if I could go. He told me that he didn't care what I did.

We finally arrived at my brother's house that evening; I got dressed and waited on my cousin to pick me up. It was two hours later than the time we were to have left for the party. Willie started to rant about how he wasn't going to let me disrespect other people's houses by going out and coming back at an indecent hour. My brother's wife responded to his rants and said it was all right. They gave me the keys to the house and I left anyway, but I told my cousin to promise me that she would have me back by 1:00 a.m. When we arrived at the club, I couldn't even enjoy myself because I was afraid of how Willie would act when I returned.

I was at my brother's house at 1:30 a.m. My cousin went back to the party. When I walked into the house, I was hoping that Willie was asleep, but he wasn't. I saw him pacing the floor. The first thing he said was that he didn't like what I did, and if I had to go through all of that to be with a man out there, I should've stayed out there with him. I knew that my family heard what he said to me. I decided then to keep the peace and keep my mouth shut. I was so embarrassed. I went on to the bedroom and sat in the chair watching TV and crying the rest of the night. Willie sat up the rest of the night in the den watching TV. The next

68

morning when everyone got up, he started fussing. It really hurt me very badly because my two nieces and Jamar were there looking on. I told him that he should have stayed home. Willie packed his bags and left. I tried to cover up for him and let everyone know that he was suffering from PTSD. I felt they didn't understand and judged us.

To my surprise, Willie called a couple days later and told me that he was coming back to bring us home. He said he planned to stay at the nearby military base. I shared I had already rented a car and to pick us up from the rental office when we got home. When he came to pick us up, he acted like nothing happened.

I was still troubled about his behavior during our visit with my family, so I brought it up. That was a great mistake on my part. He started fussing at me. I asked him to stop arguing in front of Jamar. Willie darted after me, balled his fist, and screamed at me, to shut up. He told me he would not tolerate disrespect. Before I knew it, he hit me on the side of my head with his fist. I fell to the floor. Jamar started screaming and crying. I managed to pick myself up off the floor and dialed 911.

The police told me that I could file charges. I opted not to thinking things had calmed down. My son and I went to his room and locked the door in order to stay out of Willie's sight. Minutes later, I heard Willie coming up the stairs; he looked in all the rooms and saw that I was nowhere to be found. He came to Jamar's bedroom door, jiggled the knob and asked me to open the door. I replied that we were afraid of him. I pleaded with him to leave us alone. He finally kicked the door open.

When he came through the door, I sat quietly, afraid to say anything. Jamar started crying again and Willie told him to shut up. He then told me that he didn't appreciate the fact that I called the cops. He didn't even apologize for what he did. Out of fear, Jamar and I did not sleep that night.

A couple days later during my lunch break; I stopped by the police station to see about filing charges. I told the sheriff about Willie's PTSD. He said based on his mental state, he could serve a warrant for his arrest and admit him into the psychiatric ward. This required that Willie and I both be home. I also needed to get his mental health physician to sign documents stating the status of Willie's mental health in order to get the police department to pick Willie up whenever he had an out break or crisis.

The next day, I went to the VA hospital, talked with his physician, and told her everything that happened. She confirmed what the sheriff said. The only thing she could do was to put him on some different medications and continue his therapy sessions. My fears set in; I couldn't go through with it. I knew that they couldn't keep him there forever. The thought of what would happen when he came home overwhelmed me. Before I left, she asked me why I stayed in the relationship with him. I told her that even though I couldn't change him or fix the problem, I loved him. I wanted him to get better and a part of me wanted to be there to see the transformation.

After that incident, I just tried to slack up calling the authorities and dealt with Willie on my own the best way I could. I was afraid that he would commit suicide or something if I had left him. It seemed that I looked out more for Willie than me and Jamar.

Chapter 6

Later on in the year, we took a cruise to the Bahamas. When I first mentioned the cruise, Willie grunted about not wanting to go because he'd gone on a cruise before. He also mentioned that it would be too much walking for him. I told him that I had never gone on one and that he was going even if I had to push him around in a wheelchair. He finally agreed. The cruise was awesome. We met some other couples there and hung out with them the whole time. The men even took turns pushing Willie in a wheelchair whenever he needed to be pushed. We went out on a tour to Paradise Island and fell in love with it. Everything we took part in was beautiful.

Willie spent one day in the room alone and watched movies, ordered room service and got pampered. I was out and about on the ship taking part in some of the activities. We had one of the best times of our lives on that cruise. He was excited and happy that he went. When it was time to leave the Bahamas, Willie wanted to go back over to Paradise Island and stay for a few more days. He told me to leave him there. Willie didn't want to go. I knew I couldn't just leave him like that. I told him that I would plan another trip by plane, so that we could spend the whole time in Paradise Island.

My birthday was approaching soon and Willie asked for Annie's phone number. I didn't ask him why he wanted it. That Friday morning before I left for work, he told me that he was taking me out that night and told me to call the 24 hour children day care center near by and make reservation for Jamar to stay there for a few hours. I did. Willie didn't tell me where he was taking me. After dropping Jamar off, Willie took me to a popular restaurant in North West Atlanta. When we walked in, I saw Annie and Cathy there awaiting our arrival. I was stunned to see them. Right then, I knew that was the reason why he asked for Annie's number. He wanted her to set up everything for him as a surprise to me. Later on at the restaurant, we had a few more friends that came in to join us. It was such a great surprise.

When we picked up Jamar, he was angry with us because we did not take him with us to celebrate my birthday. Willie made it up to him by letting him choose the restaurant he wanted to take me to the following weekend. Jamar chose Red Lobster. We had a blast there also.

Willie began to not clean up behind himself. He would leave dirty clothes lying on the floor and dirty dishes in the sink. Another problem I had with Willie was he leaving the house at a moment's notice. I'd ask him where he was going and he told me that he never liked anyone to ask where he was going. I would get upset and worry. I told him that it wasn't good for him not to tell me where he was going. I did not care if it was right around the corner. I felt anything could happen out there in the street and I would not know how to start telling the authorities. To be honest, I was afraid of him driving to the corner store. I had to get

73

used to the fact that he would never let me know his whereabouts at times. He usually called me after arriving at his destination to tell me where he was.

Outside of other things, Willie became impotent, a weakness and inability of the male to achieve or maintain an erection. My heart hurt as Willie started to think that he was less of a man. We both were very distraught about his impotency. Willie's physicians, Dr. Jones and Dr. Crawford told us that Willie's impotency could have come from some of the medications he was taking for his medical conditions. They also told Willie that smoking cigarettes, being stressed out, and angry all the times could affect his impotency. I certainly didn't want him to get off his medications, so I asked the physicians what else could be done. She recommended an erectile device. She ordered it for him and he began to use it. It was a frustrating thing for Willie, but he used it nonetheless that is until he really got fed up with it one night. He told me that he had a remedy for that problem.

I found out a few days later when he said that he was trying to prove a point that the doctors were right about the meds causing his impotency. I almost hit the ceiling because that could only mean that he didn't take his meds. I warned him about the effects that could have on his overall health and attitude if he stopped taking his meds. Fortunately, Willie started back taking his medications. I worked with him a lot on his impotency in every way possible, because I did not want that to dampen his spirit or to make him feel worthless.

Jamar had another problem with his conduct at school. We received a report that he hit another student and he was

74

disobeying the teachers. When we got home that evening, I told Willie about it and he got highly upset. Willie took off his belt and Jamar came running and screaming to me. I stood in the middle of them and told Willie that he should try conversing with Jamar instead of whipping him.

Willie got mad and told me that since I wouldn't let him raise Jamar how he wanted to, he was leaving the house for the weekend and we could do whatever we wanted.

Jamar and I came home that Friday evening and saw that Willie had left. I started to worry again. I hoped he'd call to let me know he was all right. Later that night, he did just that. He told me that he drove to Columbia, SC, got a hotel room and was getting ready to go out and get something to eat. He gave me the number to his room. I called him a few hours later to make sure he'd gotten settled in. He said that he was reading his Bible and meditating. He told me that he was going to go visit the military base the next morning.

He returned home on Sunday. He seemed revitalized from his trip. He sat down to eat and told me about his trip. He brought back a Children's Bible for Jamar and a new bible for me. Jamar asked him where he'd gone. Willie replied that he just needed to go away to clear his mind.

My sister-in-law, Althea and a friend of hers came to visit us the following weekend. Althea and Willie studied the Bible most of her stay. She asked me before they left, how Willie was doing since the incident that took place at her home. I told her that Willie was still acting out which was a continuous thing for him to do because of the PTSD. Althea told me that she was going to talk with him. Before they left, we all prayed together. Jamar and I stood in the driveway as they drove off. When they were out of sight, Willie came out of the garage and pounded his fist on the trashcan telling me that he didn't appreciate me talking about him to Althea. I told him that I wasn't talking him down in any way. I just wanted her to help him see my side of things since he never listened to me. He told me that since I had so much to tell her, I should've packed my bags and left with them. I didn't say another word; instead, I just walked away and let him fuss.

Willie had cooled down by the evening and took Jamar and me out to eat. I excused myself to the restroom. On my way back to our table, I noticed that Willie had on mixed matched socks, one colorful and the other black. I told him, and asked how he'd managed to do that. Rather than answer my question, he asked me why I let him come out of the house looking like that. He started up a big fuss about how I needed to learn how to get his clothes right after I washed them. I told him I didn't know how the socks got mixed up because I always place them how they should be. I figured it had to be his doings. I prayed that Willie would immediately finish dragging this out—He was angry into the next evening.

During one conversation Linda and I had about her father, I told her that he had hit me during a heated rage. She asked why I'd stayed with him. I told her that I loved him and that he was not a well man and I just couldn't turn my back on him. Linda shared that when Willie was with her mother, he used to cause so much pain, heartaches and tears with his raging, fussing and anger at times.

I started detecting that it was bothering Willie a lot because he did not see much of Linda and her son, plus she and Willie were not communicating well. One day I took it upon myself and wrote Linda a letter and took it over to her job where she worked part-time. She had not arrived yet, so I left it under her office door assuming that she would have gotten it. She never mentioned anything to me about it.

I figured I would write the letter to her explaining the situation about her father suffering from PTSD and depression. I was thinking that she didn't have too much interest in coming around him because she might have never known that her father was mentally ill and did not like his behavior and was ashamed of him. That could have been the reason why she seemed to have kept her distance, thinking of her haunting past experiences growing up in the same household with Willie.

When Linda mentioned on the phone one day about the pain she suffered from her father, I pretty much knew right then that she did not know why the relationship with him was so stormy, and furthermore, he did not know at the time what was wrong with himself when he acted out like that. I figured that she didn't know what was wrong with him and anyone else experiencing his behavior probably did not know either. I was trying to get the point over to her in the letter by letting her know what was going on with her father's mental health status. Willie's physicians said that PTSD, which brought on depression, was the primary reason for his explosive behavior and his acting out after the war to the present time. I did not want her to stay away from her father thinking negative things against him, even if she did not want to be around Jamar and me. If that was the case, I wanted her to know how mentally challenged he was and try to accept him for who he was a little bit more. I definitely wanted her to understand that Willie's bad behavior and his actions were not done intentionally to hurt anyone.

The letter that I left for Linda explained her father's PTSD condition. It also included information about Agent Orange, PTSD, and a book for kids about PTSD that was given to Willie from one of the mental health doctors at the VA, called, "Why Is Daddy Like He Is?" It contained information for children whose parents suffered from PTSD. The book shares the effects of the disorder from a child's point of view.

I prayed and hoped that this information, included in the letter to Linda, made sense to her and that she would understand why her father acted the way he did at times.

I came in from work one evening and Willie told me that he almost set the house on fire. I was shocked. I asked him how? He told me that he was trying to light the fireplace and a great gulf of smoke came out and set of all the smoke alarms. It was enough smoke for the fire trucks to come out. Thankfully, our fire alarm was connected to our alarm system. The trucks came out immediately. Another incident, Willie almost set the house on fire when he put some sausage links into a cooking pot, went in the living room to watch television and fell asleep. The pot went dry of water and started burning. The fire truck came because of the fire alarm went off. I was so happy that the house didn't catch on fire and thankful that nothing happened to Willie. I fussed with him so much about leaving the stove unattended while cooking.

Chapter 7

Willie decided that he wanted to get away from Jamar and me for a few days. He said that he was going to go to New Orleans for Mardi Gras. He asked me to call around to some hotels and make a reservation for him. I was worried about him driving all by himself so I decided to call some of his friends and family members to see if they would accompany him. Unfortunately, none of them was available to go.

Willie was sitting across from me at the kitchen table that evening when I began calling for reservations for him. The hotels that I called, I told him that all of them were booked up, even though a few of them had vacancies. I did not want him to take that trip by himself and definitely not driving alone. He wasn't supposed to be driving those distances like that. He was just doing whatever came to his mind and not thinking about the consequences. I lied to Willie hoping that he wouldn't take the trip anyway. Fortunately, my trickery was what kept him from taking that trip all alone.

He told me that he wished he hadn't told me where he was going because it seemed like I brought bad luck on him because he was unable to book a room. When I started questioning him, he started getting frustrated, yelling at me and telling me to shut up because I was always messing something up. He didn't speak to me for two days. I didn't care that he did not speak to me. I was just happy he did not go on that highway and mix with the type of crowd I knew would be there.

One week later, I came home and found that Willie had packed some luggage and had gone without leaving a note or anything. I became so worried. I hated when he did things like that. I knew he did things like that just to prove a point to me that he was a man that could travel alone without anything happening. I began calling around to different friends and family members and I finally caught up with him at my brother Eugene's home in Charleston, SC. When my brother handed Willie the phone, he laughed and said that he knew that it wouldn't be long before I found him.

He told me that he'd be staying there for a couple days and that my sister-in-law Althea would be taking him to the Christian Bookstore to purchase a study bible like the one she had when she visited us. He must have forgotten that he had already sent the money to her to get the study bible and for her to ship it to him.

Willie started forgetting a lot of things. One day he suggested we put a fence up around our house. I agreed that it would be a good idea. A few days later, I saw Willie talking to two men outside our home. When he came into the house, he said that the men were willing to place our fence up but the price was too steep so he didn't think he'd use them.

Saturday morning, I saw the same two men outside our home with a truck pulling out the materials to build the fence. Willie said that he hadn't authorized the men to do anything. He went outside and exchanged words with the men and they left. They were pretty upset. He said later on that the owner of the company said that he was going to make him pay for their time coming out to our house and getting the materials together. Willie was telling other people to do things and then not remembering what he was telling them. We got the fence put up for a more reasonable price later on.

Willie had his own ideas of protection. On our way to Orlando, Florida for a family trip, Willie stopped at a gun shop. I knew he couldn't be buying a gun but became curious after his lengthy time inside the shop. I got out the car and went inside. When I saw that Willie had just completed a transaction to buy a gun, I became hysterical. I asked Willie why he bought the gun. He said that the highways and the world were becoming more dangerous and we needed protection. I replied that God has always protected us and we didn't need a gun. I asked the clerk could my husband get his money back. The clerk said he could but only if he wanted to. I was really afraid of him having a gun at home because of his rages. He could have easily snapped and harmed us with it. He had an old gun, but it wasn't working. He would not listen to me.

Willie told me that he wasn't going to return the gun so I might as well rest my case. I did, but not before telling him that he would have to leave the gun in the garage, because I didn't want it in the house. I couldn't enjoy my time in Florida because of my worrying.

The first incident we had with the gun that made me petrified was when Willie picked up Jamar from school and met me at my job to take him to a doctor's appointment. When I opened the back door of the car for Jamar to get out, I saw the gun on the floor where it had slid down from under the driver's seat. I blasted Willie. I told him having the gun was very dangerous. I stressed that Jamar could have easily picked up the gun and played with it and it could have went off. I told Willie if I ever see that gun out like that again, I was going to get rid of it. Willie responded that I'd better not do such a thing, because if I did, I would have hell on my hands.

The next day, I noticed that Willie had placed the gun in his briefcase and placed it in his car trunk. However, that didn't put my mind at ease. Because of the PTSD and depression, I was also afraid he'd shoot someone if they made him mad enough or cause someone to shoot him.

My heart dropped into the pit of my stomach the day Willie told me that he was leaving and taking Jamar with him on a trip to Bush Gardens. I begged and pleaded with him not to take Jamar with him. He couldn't be trusted to do the simple things around the house with Jamar, much less left alone in another state. Willie could not see or hear well and was definitely not detail oriented. Thankfully, a friend of his went along with them. His friend helped him drive the entire trip going and coming back. His friend stayed with one of his relatives that lived there in the city. Willie and Jamar stayed at the hotel.

I was relieved when they finally got back into town in one piece. I didn't know what they did on the trip nor did I ask right away, I saw that Willie was exhausted and Jamar was whinny and cranky. When Willie went to lie down, I asked Jamar what they had done on their trip. Jamar said that he had gone on some rides at the park and a little site seeing around the city. He said that his father had pulled over on a busy interstate and urinated. Jamar said that he was afraid because there were big tractor-trailers zooming by which shook the car while he was in the back seat.

He also admitted that while at a restaurant, Willie had locked the keys in the car and they had to wait two hour for road assistance. I decided then that I would never let Willie go away with Jamar again if I could help it.

One Saturday morning, Willie asked me to go with him shopping. I looked around for clothes while he bought some suits. I went to other stores near by. When I returned, I saw Willie getting the suits he'd bought tailored. I walked up to him and asked him why he'd bought suits that were the same style and color as the ones he had in the closet at home. I told him that people would think he's wearing the same clothes repeatedly. He got so angry and yelled at me in front of the other shoppers. He said that he didn't care what I or anybody else thought about his clothes. He said he'd wished he didn't invite me to come along. I ended up taking Jamar and walking out of the store in tears. He asked yet again, why was his father so angry? I just told him that he got upset and angry because I asked him about the clothing that he bought. When Willie came out of the store, the look on his face showed me that he had it in for me. We got into the car and he fussed all the way home. We were supposed to stop by a restaurant to eat but he forgot   and   I   didn't   bother   reminding   him.

When we got home, I prepared something quick to

eat, because we all were hungry. I cooked hot dogs and made baked beans. Willie was upset when he saw the food I had prepared. He said to me that he was not about to eat no slop like that. He stormed out the house and came back an hour later with a dinner from the restaurant. Afterwards, he fell asleep watching the television. I was so glad that Willie went to sleep. He'd slept for three or four hours and when he woke up, he was like a brand new person. It looked as if he'd slept his anger away.

Sunday morning came and Willie was irritated because Jamar and I were not ready for church. I was fixing breakfast and Jamar was still upstairs putting on his clothes. Willie said that he didn't want to be late for church because he needed to get his handicap parking space. I hurried and finished breakfast and went upstairs to help Jamar get ready. As soon as I did, I heard Willie leaving out the house. I ran downstairs and told him that we'd be out shortly but he left anyway.

Jamar and I left out about five minutes after Willie left. When we arrived at the church, we saw Willie turning into the church parking lot. We ended up parking right across from where Willie parked his car. Jamar and I caught up with him so that we could enter the church and sit together. I whispered to Willie that I didn't like what he'd done and he stormed at me very loudly saying that he didn't appreciate the fact that I made him late and he wasn't able to get his usual parking space. People began to stare at us. I was so embarrassed. Jamar and I sat elsewhere in the church because Willie said that he didn't want to sit next to a stupid ignorant person like me. I just shook my head, sighed and prayed silently. When Jamar and I got home, I started cooking dinner. Willie came in a little while after us and began arguing again. I ignored him for the rest of the evening. I had the word of God singing in my heart.

Through the rest of the week, Willie's behavior faired well. I found out about a concert that would be going on that weekend. I told him that a few singing artists would be performing at the Chastain Park and I asked if he wanted to go. He immediately accepted my invitation. The day of the concert, Willie and I bought food and drinks to take out there and ended up sharing some of it with a couple sitting at the table with us. We had a great time. The music just sang to his mind and soul. It made me happy to see him enjoying himself.

Willie got angry yet again that following Saturday. When I entered the house, he said that he was mad because I was gone half the day to the barbershop to get Jamar's hair cut. I told him that we stayed longer so I could sign up Jamar for a hair contest. There was a nationally known hair product company at the barbershop taking pictures of the children's haircuts. The winner would model their hair products and get $1,000. Willie didn't approve of me entering Jamar in the contest and told me that he didn't like his haircut anyway.

Willie started fussing so badly that he told me to pack my bags and leave. I asked him to pack his bags and leave. He told me that I just wanted him to leave so I could bring my man to the house. I told him to stop accusing me of stuff like that. I started to think that someone must have been in his life before me that wasn't trustworthy, and now I was probably paying for someone else's sin. I didn't leave, so he left the house. I prayed he'd be okay.

A few weeks later, the hair products company called and said that out of two or three hundred children, Jamar was the runner up in the contest and was entitled to receive $500. I received the money for him approximately three weeks later. I was so elated that Jamar had won. I was hoping that the company would have given Jamar a modeling contract.

It was time for Willie's six to eight week stay in the VA hospital again. Willie told me that he wasn't going because the meds were making him impotent among other things. He asked me what else I wanted to go wrong with him. I replied that I didn't want anything to go wrong with him and that he needed to go because the meds make him calmer. Willie treated me like a queen when he was in a good mood. I wanted him to feel good about himself and not make himself or the family miserable. I was tired of the tearful nights Jamar and I shared. The only peace I found was in the company of my co-workers and my work. However, the tearful nights got so bad that my eyes were always puffy and even my co-workers jokingly asked if my husband had punched me in the eyes? I would just tell a lie and tell them that they were puffy because of the lack of sleep.

Jamar found peace at his school among his peers. He never wanted to miss a day. He'd throw a tantrum if I ever came to pick him up early for some reason. To do us both a favor, on our way home sometimes, I'd drive past the house just to delay seeing Willie a little longer, because I didn't know what kind of mood he was in.

Jamar's behavior continued to keep me back and forth at his school speaking with his teachers and counselors. They advised me to take him to get tested to see if he had ADD or ADHD (Attention Deficit Disorder or (Attention Deficit Hyperactivity Disorder). I got a referral from Jamar's pediatrician to see the psychologist and took him. A couple weeks later, I received a call from the psychologist's office asking that Willie and I stop in so he could go over Jamar's test results with us together.

When we arrived, the psychologist told us that Jamar was diagnosed with a mild case of ADD. I knew what the terms meant but Willie didn't. He asked the doctor to break it all down for him. He told him what it meant explaining all of the different level of behaviors. He told us that Jamar's main behaviors were trouble paying attention, fidgety, short attention span and not listening. He told us that he recommended Jamar being put on a mild dose of medication called Ritalin and that he would give us a prescription for it and to follow up with him in about three months. After the psychologist finished his explanation and mentioned the medication, Willie stood up, stumped his cane while walking on the floor, and said that there was no way he'd place his child on medication just to make the teachers happy and anyone else. He turned and looked me in the face and asked me why I dragged him there to waste his time with that bunch of foolishness? He told the doctor to take the results and flush them down the toilet.

Willie walked toward the door, looked back at me and told me if I wanted a ride back home, I'd better come on or find another way. He added that he had a remedy to the situation and that was to get Jamar out of that school immediately.

In no time, Jamar was transferred to our church private school. It was Willie's decision. He said that he was sick and tired of me going through all of that with the teachers and the counselors going up there constantly for something Jamar did or did not do from the previous school. He said that he'd eat bread and drink water if he had to in order to pay for the schooling.

Funny thing, Jamar stayed on the Honor Roll and Principal's list at the new school. None of the teachers there had any problems with him whatsoever. When we would see his teachers, they would tell us how intelligent, knowledgeable and creative Jamar was. We had no more problems out of him since he started school there. It was definitely a great relief on Willie and me. A week before my birthday, Willie told me to pack my bags. I asked him where were we going, but he didn't answer. I didn't know what type of clothes to pack; I pretty much got an idea based on some of the clothes he'd packed for himself.

Off to Columbus GA, we went to visit one of his army buddies and his wife who were celebrating their 30th year wedding anniversary. We left Jamar with my cousin Debra during our trip. Willie and I had a fun argument free night. He blew my mind the way he bragged about me to his friends and called me little pet names. I thought to myself, 'if they only knew some of the things that went on in our home and how he treated me behind closed doors.

I suggested to Willie that it would be nice to celebrate our ten-year wedding anniversary when it came around. He didn't say anything. I figured it was for the best. On our way back home, I drove over a pothole in the road. I didn't see it, but that didn't matter to Willie. He ruined a perfectly good weekend by fussing at me about how I couldn't drive and that I was messing up his car. He finally told me to pull over and give him the keys. He fussed the rest of the way home. He told me that he wasn't going to let me drive again. When we got home, I let him have it and it seemed that the lack of argument from over the weekend came out that night. I left to pick Jamar up from Debra's house.

I arrived at Debra's and all I said to her when she asked how the trip went was that it was lovely. She'd informed me that Jamar and her kids had just popped in a movie. I knew Jamar wouldn't want to leave, so against my better judgment, I sat around until the movie ended. I got home a couple hours later and Willie started with his same old script of accusing me. I told him to ask Jamar what went on. Willie told me that he wasn't asking Jamar anything and that he didn't want me to start up his career of cover-ups and lies. I just left him downstairs fussing and I went upstairs to the bedroom to do some things.

Jamar detected that I was crying and he asked me again why his dad was so angry when I did not do anything wrong. I finally told Jamar that his dad was suffering from a mental disorder from the war that caused him to be that way. I started reading over the information, the book on "Why is daddy like he is? By reading the information to him, I was hoping that he would understand his dad a little bit better when he goes through his crises. Either way it was still hard for us when Willie would go through it. Sometimes it was so painful, that I, myself forget that he had PTSD and depression. I told Jamar to pray for his father every day and ask God to heal his mind.

When Willie sometimes went into one of his modes, I really didn't know what to do. It seemed as if I had a decision to make. Should I stay or should I leave? That was one question I agonized about with God constantly.

One Sunday evening, Willie had a bout with burping and chest pains after eating dinner that I'd prepared. Alarmed, I insisted on calling the EMS. He was adamant and didn't want me calling anybody. I had to do something because it didn't seem like it was getting any better, so I rushed to the store, bought some anti-acid medication, and gave it to him. It got a little better and he was able to sleep some but I didn't sleep at all.

When I left for work the next day, Willie was doing fine. He had stopped the burping and had no more chest pains. Around mid-morning, Willie called to my work place. When I answered the phone, all he could say to me that I needed to come home quickly because the pain started back and they were real sharp and he was gasping telling me to please hurry. I was so afraid that he was having a heart attack. I began shouting in the office that my husband needed help and I needed to go home.

My co-workers called 911 and gave them my home address. I had to call Willie back to let him know to open the door if he could and that the EMS was on the way. One of my co-workers rushed me home. When we arrived to the house, the paramedics were just about to drive off taking Willie to the hospital. I was so elated that Willie was able to open the door at home, because if he didn't, the paramedics would have had to knock the door down to get in. At the hospital, the ER Cardiologist ordered some tests to be done along with EKG testing. It showed an abnormal

EKG that suggests a possible mild heart attack. Willie was admitted into the hospital.

The next day, Willie was assigned to Dr. Moore, a cardiologist. Just prior to Willie's discharge from the hospital that evening after about a week stay, the doctor showed us x-rays and other tests of Willie's heart. The films showed stenosis (narrowing or constriction of the heart vessels). He also had Arteriosclerosis (thickening of the walls around the arteries) and was diagnosed with Coronary Artery Disease (CAD). Dr. Moore explained that the blockages were possibly from plaques built up from smoking cigarettes, and elevated cholesterol that caused improper blood flow that could be conducive to heart attacks and other heart problems, even strokes. Luckily Dr. Moore dissolved the plaques without performing any surgery on Willie.

Dr. Moore told Willie to quit smoking, the same thing I have been telling him for a long time.

Willie looked at him, smiled and said, 'Okay, Doc.'

Dr. Moore told Willie, that the cigarettes he smoked before his chest pains started should be his last ones he smoked.

While I went to get the car, a medical assistant wheeled Willie down outside for me to pick him up and assist him in the car. As we were leaving the hospital driveway, Willie asked me to stop by the gas station down the street. I thought maybe he wanted to get something to drink; instead, he ended up asking me to buy him some cigarettes. I looked at him and asked him if he thought I was a fool or something. I replied no. I added that if I were him I wouldn't want to look at another cigarette after all

91

he'd been through and that he really must want to die. Willie said that he'd be all right. I told him that if he wanted some cigarettes that bad, he would have to get them the best way he could.

When we got home, our next-door neighbor was outside washing his car. He stopped in order to help Willie out of the car. He asked Willie how he was feeling. I heard Willie say that he was feeling okay, but he needed him to do him a favor when he was done with his car.

I asked Willie when we got in the house what favor he needed that he couldn't get me to do. Willie got an attitude and said that I didn't have to know everything. He then went into the garage and waited until our neighbor came. I overheard their conversation and saw the transaction that took place. Willie gave him some money and told him that he wanted two packs of cigarettes. Our neighbor gave Willie the money back. He said that he was sorry and that he would not go behind my back and buy cigarettes knowing that Willie had been in the hospital for about a week because of chest pain. He was afraid of doing that.

Our neighbor left. Willie was so determined to have his cigarettes to the point that he got in his car and drove to the store and bought not just two packs of cigarettes but a whole carton.

Willie constantly stayed on my back about buying him cigarettes when I grocery shopping or just stopping to any store. I kept telling him no. He hated when I reminded him of the doctor's advice. Dr. Moore was not the only one to tell him about quit smoking. All of his doctors told him the same thing. Willie's cravings had gotten worse. He called me one rainy evening before I got off from work and told me to stop and purchase him a pack of cigarettes because he didn't want to go out in the bad weather himself. When I got home, I didn't know how to tell him that I didn't buy what he wanted, but I told him anyway.

He became furious and he told me that he always did what I asked him to do but he'd never again do anything I asked. I said; if that's the way you want to be toward me because of some cigarettes then just let it be that way.

Chapter 8

One of my great aunts from South Carolina passed away. Willie loved her because she made him laugh a lot every time we saw her. We attended her funeral. After the funeral, family and friends went to her house for dinner.

Willie and one of my cousins, who was also a Vietnam War veteran, suffering from PTSD and depression, were talking and trading war stories. When Willie got up to mingle with other family members, I went to my cousin and told him what I was experiencing with Willie's behavior and that Willie was diagnosed with PTSD. I asked him what he did to cope with the disorder. He told me that he took his meds faithfully and tried to keep a positive outlook about himself and the people around him. I asked if he would discreetly talk to Willie about PTSD, and if Willie seemed okay with the conversation, please encourage him to do what he was doing in order to cope with it.

Watching from across the room, I saw that he might have been mentioning PTSD to Willie, as Willie's demeanor seemed to change. I overheard Willie tell him that he does take his meds, but sometimes he slacks up on them because of the way they make him feel; mostly sluggish, feeling groggy, no energy to do anything. Willie went on to tell him that he could hardly function, and it made him have all kinds of crazy thoughts. Willie stated that he did not want to live the rest of his life being doped up like that. My cousin told Willie that the medication he took was the only way he was able to function. Willie got a little irritated with him and told him that they were two different people and what affected him may not affect someone else the same way. Willie asked him to change the subject of conversation.

I thought at times that Willie didn't want to take his meds because he thought he would miss a moment in life or lose control in some way. From my point of view, he definitely was in control of everything in our lives. When I mentioned the meds to him, he often replied that I wanted him to take his meds so that he could be knocked out so I would be able to go and see another man. There was just no getting through to him sometimes.

Days later, Willie started having a sharp pain in the back of his head. He'd move his head from side to side to alleviate the pain. I told him that he definitely needed to get seen by his doctor and get it checked out. He refused to go. A week later, he went to the VA hospital for an appointment and ran into one of his military buddies and he told Willie about another veteran that he knew passed away recently from a brain aneurism. Willie came home and asked me what an aneurism was and what kind of symptoms one may have. I told him basically the same symptoms that he was having; pain in his head. When I told him that, he got really scared and told me to hurry up and make him an appointment to see the doctor. Dr. Crawford saw Willie and ordered a head scan to be done on him. The test result came back normal. She ended up changing his blood pressure and cholesterol medications. Fortunately after the change in medications, he didn't complain anymore about the head pain.

One day I came home and again found Willie has hired someone to work on the house. This time, they were laying a wood floor from the front door down the hallway to the kitchen. I went directly to the garage where Willie was smoking a cigarette. Upset, I stated that he should have talked to me before hiring the men. He looked at me and said that he didn't have to do anything. We ended up having another heated argument. Willie told me that if I didn't like what he did, then I could leave.

I couldn't cook because the kitchen floor was being worked on so Jamar and I went out to eat. I was really upset with Willie. I was in tears and said to myself that I was not going to take him nothing back home to eat because of what he did and said to me.

When I got home, the workers had already left. I found Willie to be in a good mood. He said that the floor would look good when finished. He then asked me what I'd brought him back to eat. I couldn't believe he asked me that and told me earlier that I could leave and don't come back. Fortunately, I had bought him something to eat, if I didn't, it may have set him off in a rage.

During Father's Day weekend, we took a family trip down to Selma Alabama to visit two of his brothers and their families. On our way back home from the trip, we were driving on the interstate when I informed Willie that he was going the wrong way. He got angry with me, telling me that he knew where he was going and that he had a map in the car, and didn't need my input. I kept silent and let Willie do what he thought was right. Meanwhile, Jamar was sitting in the back seat shivering from the wind blowing through the window in his face, plus Willie had the air conditioning on full blast. This didn't make any sense to me. It was late in the evening. I knew that Jamar was afraid to ask his dad to roll up the window. I didn't want to say anything, so I kept looking in the back seat at him trying to signal to him to speak up and ask his dad to roll up the window. Jamar kept shaking his head telling me no under his breath.

Willie saw what I was doing and said that if I look back one more time he was going to stop the car and make me get in the back seat with Jamar. I deliberately looked back again and Willie stopped the car. When I got in the back seat, I laid Jamar's head in my lap and placed my arms over him to block the wind. After about twenty minutes, Willie finally let the window up.

Willie had driven thirty miles out of the way before he realized that he needed to get directions from someone other than me. He stopped at a McDonalds Restaurant and told us that if we needed to use the rest room, then we'd better do it right then because he wasn't going to stop until we reached home. Fortunately, when I came out of the rest room, Willie was talking to a man who apparently had been in the military judging by their conversation. Willie introduced us and I asked if he wanted me to drive the rest of the way home. I was shocked when he gave me the keys.

When we got back in the car, Willie had a brand new attitude. He was refreshed and we talked about our trip in a calm manner. I was thankful to God for the moment of relief.

Willie was a strange man at times. It seemed like he couldn't distinguish between respect and disrespect. For example, one day Willie told Jamar to clean his room. Jamar responded and told his father that he had already cleaned his room. Willie got so mad that he tried to whip Jamar stating that he was talking back at him. He walked fast toward Jamar with his belt raised and I stepped in between them and told Jamar to run. I dared Willie to put his hands on Jamar or me. I told him that if he did, one of us was going down, either him or me. Willie told me that since I wouldn't let him raise his son, then I had better do something about Jamar. I asked what was it that I needed to do since Jamar didn't do anything wrong? I told him that I didn't think that any one could raise a child by yelling and lashing out at them like he did. I told him that since his PTSD treatment session was coming up again, he really needed to go. He did not want me to mention that to him. He blasted me out because I had.

Jamar's school had a parent breakfast. I couldn't go because of an important meeting at work. I told Jamar that I would ask his father to go. Jamar immediately expressed his displeasure; he told me that he didn't want his daddy to come because he was afraid he'd embarrass him in some kind of way. I pleaded with Jamar to allow Willie to go with him. Jamar finally gave in and said that it was okay for him to go.

When I got home that evening, Jamar greeted me at the garage door. Willie had picked him up after school. Before we went in the house, I asked Jamar about the

98

breakfast. He said that he and his dad had a great time. All of Jamar's teachers had given him a great report. He told me that his dad had taken him to Red Lobster because he was being such a good boy in school. I was thankful to God that everything went well. When I got in the house and went to the kitchen, I saw that Willie had a steak and lobster dinner that he purchased for me.

Willie was in a good mood. He told me that he really enjoyed talking with Jamar's teachers and the principal. I thought to myself that the outing was good for him. It was better than him sitting around the house smoking all the time finding things to stress and fuss about. Jamar and I were Willie's primary targets. Whenever I suggested that he go somewhere, if it was just to a friend house to talk, he would tell me that it seemed as if I wanted him away from the house or I didn't want to be married to him anymore. I assured him that was not true. I only wanted to see him happy.

My brother's daughter, Bridgett came to stay the summer with us to do her internship for college. Of course, I was afraid of how Willie would act. Bridgett had already experienced a taste of Willie's behavior in the past; I really didn't want her to experience Willie behavior for a whole summer. Since we agreed for her to stay, I just constantly prayed to the Lord that he would do well.

The Lord worked it out so that Bridgett spent a lot of time out with a friend some evenings after work. During the times Willie lashed out at me, she would be either gone out or in her bedroom asleep.

During Bridgett's stay, we went to a 4th of July celebration. It was at a park and a lot of people were there enjoying the festivities. While we were there, a man walked by us and by mistake, stepped on Willie's foot. Willie looked at the man and asked him did he see his foot there? The man apologized, but Willie kept it going. He told the man that if he needed to walk in his direction again, he had better find another way of getting there. The man gave him a very cold look. I was afraid and too embarrassed to say anything. Bridgett and the people around me were looking at us and I felt so small. Nevertheless, I thanked God for the grace and mercy that he granted me while Bridgett was with us. She did not experience the worst side of him like she did at their house in SC.

A few days later, Willie and I were at a gas station and he and another man were aiming to get to the same pump but the other man got there before we did. Willie got out his car and said to the man that he was wrong for pulling up at that pump first. I tried to tell him that the man had the right of way, and Willie yelled at me telling me to shut up. Willie kept talking and said to the man that some niggers don't know how to act. When he said that, the man came angrily toward him with one of his fists balled up ready to hit Willie. I yelled out to the man pleading to him not to hit my husband because he was not well.

The man stopped in his tracks and said to me that I'd better take Willie somewhere and get him well before someone hurt him because he was about to knock him out. I told Willie that he could've gotten all of us hurt out there by acting the way he did. Willie just brushed it all off like it was nothing and said that if the man had put his hands on him, he was going to pull out his gun and shoot him. I told him that the man was going to have him in a position where he would not be able to get his gun. All I could do is encourage him not to do that ever again. I knew what I said went through one ear and out the other.

A few weeks later, Willie and I were traveling to a resort hotel in New Orleans for vacation. I drank too much liquid and I had to stop to use the restroom frequently. Willie got mad and said that if I stop one more time, he was going to make me turn the car around and go back home. I asked why he would do something like that just because I needed to relieve myself. He told me that I should have known better than to drink so much fluid, and the way it looked if I kept going, we were never going to get anywhere.

We were about an hour away from our destination and I had to use the restroom again really bad. I tried to hold it as best as I could but I thought of something clever to say and I told Willie that I was sleepy and tired and I needed to wash my face with some cold water. He allowed me to stop and even told me that he'd drive the rest of the way.

The next day, I went to the fitness room and got on the treadmill. I guess I'd stayed on there too long and I got very exhausted and weak like I was going to pass out. There were two women in there that came over to assess and tend to me. They wanted to contact Willie, but I told them not to right away and that I just needed to sit awhile to see if I could get my composure back. I thanked the women and went on to my room after feeling better. Later on that night while Willie and I were watching TV, I told him what happened to me earlier. His response was that he thought I had better sense than to overexert myself like that and being a certified medical assistant as that.

The next day, we toured New Orleans and took part in a few of the activities and ate some of the delicious cuisine. Willie didn't go to the D-Day Veterans' museum while we were there. He bought me a ticket and I went in without him. I really wanted to tour that. I cried when I saw what my husband and other veterans had endured while at war.

The next day, Willie and I went to Biloxi, Mississippi and spent the night at the military base nearby. We toured the area and dined at one of the famous restaurants there. We also stopped at the oceanfront to have a romantic evening as the cool breeze enveloped our bodies. Traveling back home to Georgia was good because Willie and I didn't argue. He had a lot of good memories and it didn't hurt that he slept most of the way back home.

When we returned, there was a letter in the mailbox stating that Willie needed to come to the Veteran's Hospital in Augusta, GA for his PTSD treatments. They also stated that they'd made some pertinent changes and stressed the importance of him being there, and if he couldn't get to Augusta he could attend a program at the VA in Decatur, GA. Willie looked over the letter briefly and threw it across the table and it ended up falling on the floor. I picked it up to read it. He said that he wasn't going anywhere and that they could save their energy, paper, and time. I asked him why he didn't want to go. Willie responded by saying, he didn't want to go to either one of the hospitals because he did not want to be pumped up on all of those medications, be experimented on, or die from all of the medicines. I tried to convince him to go and that he was not going to die from the meds. I reminded him of the times that he'd gone and it didn't kill him. He suggested to me that I go in his place so I could feel what it was like since it seemed like I wanted him to go so badly. I told Willie, as far as I could see, his PTSD was taking over him and controlling his mind making him think that he did not need any help.

When I said that, Willie snatched the letter out of my hands and ripped it up. Up set, he yelled, the hell with the VAMC, the hell with all the letters they sent and the hell with me. I sat there looking at the fragments of paper in my lap as he walked way.

Willie recently had slacked up on some of his medications again. I was determined to make him take his meds properly. One Saturday afternoon, Willie went to get his car washed. When he returned, he saw that I'd laid out all his meds on the table to go over them with him so that he could take them the proper way. When he saw that, he became angry and said that I had no business tampering with his meds. I commended him on how faithful he was in taking his blood pressure, heart and diabetes meds. I told him that he needed to take his anti- depressants and PTSD meds on a regular basis the same way he did the others so he could live a more stable and happy life.

Willie said I was trying to tell him to do something all the time, then changed the subject and suggested I make a change and get my hair cut or something, because he was tired of my one style. He told me to call a beautician and get it all cut off. I asked if he was serious. He said yes and that he would pay the cost for the whole works. I wasted no time calling my beautician. I made an appointment that upcoming Saturday morning.

He gave me the money and I chose a nice short style that didn't require rollers or hot ironing. I got home four hours later and Willie was waiting for me. He loved the hairstyle and praised me for getting it cut. He didn't even complain about the length of time I was gone. He told Jamar to come and see how nice my hair looked. Jamar saw it and he liked it also saying that it was very nice. Jamar only asked why I had cut it so short and I said because his father wanted me to and that I was willing to do it.

Willie told me to get Jamar and myself ready because he wanted to go and visit one of his cousins and a friend of ours so that they could see my new hair do. Even though the excitement didn't last long because the once a week maintenance for the hairdo put a damper on everything. I had cut my hair so that my husband could see that I would do something special for him because he asked, and it made him happy. I only hoped that he'd take his meds regularly as prescribed like I had begged him to do, so that we'd all be happy and live a much more peaceful life together.

One Saturday, we went down to Macon, Georgia to visit one of Willie's uncles who was sick and ended up stopping by his father's gravesite since we were nearby. He got a little emotional and cried saying that he wished that his parents were still living. He used to bring that up every so often. Willie said that he was stationed in the military in Hawaii when he got the call about his mother passing. He said that he was shocked, emotional, in denial, and devastated. He could not believe it because he had just spoken with her the day before and she seemed to be fine. Willie, from time to time, would always predict that he would not live past fifty. I would tell him that he was not going anywhere any time soon. If anything, he would run me to my grave first. I always expressed the fact that he needed to give up the cigarettes, take all his medications as prescribed, and to try live a stress free life. Willie also often recalled the loss of his baby brother who was burned to death after their house caught fire from a wood heater. He said, apparently the heater door was not closed tightly and a piece of burning wood fell out on the floor. His mother was home with the baby alone. Unfortunately, she had stepped outside the house to do something when the house caught on fire. Willie said that she was seriously burned trying to save her child. She did survive and he and his other siblings were devastated when they received the news.

Chapter 9

Willie's daughter Linda was getting married. The night of the wedding rehearsal, Willie was shown where we would be sitting the day of the wedding. Willie escorted Linda down the isle and it was a beautiful sight to see. Everything looked lovely except our seating had changed. The night of the rehearsal, we were assigned to sit on the front row. The day of the wedding, Willie and I were seated on the second row. Willie became upset about that. He felt that the people that were sitting on the front row were not supposed to be sitting there.

Some of my relatives attended the wedding. One of them told me later on that night after the wedding that Willie was so upset to the point that he approached a couple of the people outside who were sitting on the front row telling them that they were wrong for what they did. They continued on with some cross words being said between them for a while. I was so glad when the weekend of the wedding was over.

Jamar and I were leaving the house for work and school, I said good morning to Willie and he didn't say anything to me. Jamar also said good morning. Willie did not respond to him either. When we got in the car, Jamar asked me why his father didn't say anything to him and why he looked so angry. I told him that I didn't know why. On our way home that evening, I started to feel a little down because I didn't know how Willie's mood would be. I stopped at the ice cream shop and purchased Willie a Banana Split, something that he really liked, hoping to cheer him up. When Jamar and I came home, Willie was sitting at the kitchen table. I spoke to him twice and he didn't say a word to either of us. He told me that I could eat the Banana Split or trash it for all he cared.

Jamar was feeling sad because his father didn't speak to him. I told Jamar that I was sorry for how his father was treating him. Jamar said that if he owned a car and could drive, he'd leave because he was tired of his father yelling and fussing all the time when he wasn't doing anything wrong. Later that evening, I was at the kitchen table trying to help Jamar study for a test. We always sat there because Jamar was able to concentrate better. Willie settled into the living room and turned the television on as loud as the volume could go. He was watching a movie that had a lot of profanity in it.

We tried to ignore it, but it was very interrupting to Jamar. Therefore, I politely asked Willie to lower the volume and place his hearing aids in his ear so that we could not hear it and Jamar could concentrate. He angrily turned the T.V. off, slammed the remote on the coffee table, and said that he was sick and tired of me telling him what to do. He cursed at me and told me that I should go out and find another man that I could live with or marry so that I could rule over that person. He said better yet, if I wanted a divorce, he'd sign for one the next day.

I told him that he did not have to behave like that just because I asked him to turn the volume on the TV down. I further added that Jamar needed to concentrate on studying and did not need to hear all of those profane words. Willie blurted out that in this lifetime, Jamar would be hearing a whole lot more than that before it's all over with. I pleaded with him again asking him to use his hearing aids, but he wouldn't. Willie was determined not to use them because it was something that I wanted him to do.

Jamar and I came up with an idea to use an extra remote we had lying around not being used. Jamar programmed it to the TV in the living room where Willie mostly would be. Whenever Willie would have the TV real loud, one of the two of us would turn the volume down on the TV without Willie seeing us in action. When we started doing that, Willie didn't know what was going on. A few times, he asked Jamar to come see what was going on with the TV volume automatically going down like that on its own. Jamar pretended to be checking it out and told his father that he did not know why it was doing that. We had to see what scheme we could use because we just could not take that noise. After we started doing that, Willie would use his hearing aids devices every once in a while or another TV he had.

Willie got more upset, and told us that he was going upstairs and that we'd better not bother him. When we finished downstairs, we went up stairs to prepare for bed and we heard the television in the room playing very loudly. I was afraid to approach the door to tell him yet again to turn the volume down, but when I did, I saw that our room door was locked. I knew there was no way Jamar and I were going to be able to sleep through that because Jamar bedroom was next to ours. Jamar and I went into the guest bedroom to sleep at the other end of the hall and closed the door.

I worried if I'd be able to get my clothes out for work the next day. I listened for Willie to go downstairs so I could make my move to get in the bedroom in order to get my clothes. He finally went down around mid-night in the garage to smoke his cigarettes. It was a good thing that I did go in the room when he went downstairs, because when he came back up, he went in and locked the door again. When I woke up to get ready for work, the door was still locked. I tapped on the door to tell him that we were leaving, but no response from him.

The next day, Willie was still angry. He told us that we were acting like we were trying to make him have a stroke and die. Jamar was saddened by that remark from his father and wanted to know why his father made such a remark. I could only tell him that whenever his father got upset about something, anything might come out of his mouth. The next day I told Willie that he should've been ashamed of himself saying something like that in front of Jamar. I also told him that it looked like he wanted to give me a stroke or trying to frustrate me to the point of pushing Jamar and me out of his life. Willie said if we wanted to leave, then we should leave.

I told him that we were only trying to love him the best way we could, but he couldn't see that. After that, Willie told me that if I said another word to him, he was going to pack up, leave, and find some place else to live. I did say something else to him. After that, he threw some clothes

109

and his Bible in a small overnight bag and left. I knew he'd be going somewhere to study his Bible in private and to get away from us.

When Willie returned back home the next day, he was back with the same mess again. Jamar had had enough; he asked if he could go and live with one of his friends and his parents. I told Jamar that I would work on making a better living environment for us. I was hoping that if Willie wanted a divorce from me, he'd leave. I would still worry about him because I knew he could not make it on his own. If I had left him, I would move to another state. I felt if I stayed somewhere in Georgia, he'd look for us, and there was no telling what would happen when he found us. I didn't want to put Jamar and me in more danger than what we were already going through from my own husband.

Things didn't get any better for me. The next day, I came in from work tired with very achy legs. I sat down at the kitchen table to rest before taking a shower and starting dinner. I was reading the newspaper when Willie came downstairs and saw me sitting. He asked if that was all I had to do because he was hungry and he didn't want to wait around all evening for me to cook.

I told him that I was resting. He replied that I never had to cook for him again and that he'd go out to eat everyday if he had to. I looked at him, shook my head, and went upstairs to take a shower so I could come back down and start cooking dinner. By the time I came back downstairs, Willie had already left the house. He was gone for about a couple of hours and he came back with food from Red Lobster. He said that he had already eaten and the food that he brought back was for his lunch the next day and for us not to touch it.

From that day forward, I decided to come home and start my duties regardless of how tired I was. A few days later, Willie brought home a pressure cooker, a rice steamer and a George Foreman grill that he went out and bought for me. He said that he wanted to make my life easier not having to spend so many long hours at the stove cooking. In a way, I knew he just didn't want me to have any excuses when it came to having the food done in a timely manner. The new items surely did save me time.

My class reunion was taking place at the end of the month in Charleston, SC. Willie quickly stated that he did not feel like attending. When I began to pack some clothes for Jamar and me, Willie politely asked me to pack some of his clothes also because he'd changed his mind and wanted to go along for the ride. He must have thought that I was fed up with him and was planning to leave him.

Memorial Day weekend came and we were on our way to Charleston, SC to my class reunion. Willie's car started to give us problems right after he'd gotten the oil changed earlier that morning. We stopped to get it checked at a dealership in Augusta, GA, but they were so busy that by the time they'd serviced it, we'd miss the class reunion. We just prayed and fortunately, the car got us to and from our destinations. On Friday night we had our banquet and dance. Saturday, we had a picnic at the park and Sunday we went to church service. The car got us back home that Sunday evening okay.

Willie took the car to the dealership. They kept it and gave him a Loaner's car. Two days later, they called him and told him the estimates on the work that needed to be done on the car. Willie called me while I was at work and told me that the technicians said that the repairs would cost $2,500. I became upset because I figured that they were trying to get over on Willie thinking that he didn't know any better. Willie didn't know much about cars. He was just quick to accept whatever the first shop would tell him rather than to get a second opinion. I told Willie to take the car back to the place he'd gotten the oil change and tell them that we started having problems with the car right after they serviced it. I tried to tell Willie that it could have been something simple. Willie was determined to not comply with my advice. When he called me to tell me that he was going to take the loaner's car back and decide on something to do with his car, I told him I was getting off from work within the hour and would meet him there. I did that because I did not want anyone to get over on him.

When I got to the dealership, Willie was already there and sitting at the salesman's desk. The car salesman greeted me and said that he had to step away to get the credit report. I looked at Willie cross-eyed and in disbelief. I told him that it didn't make any sense to finance another car when he only had two payments left on the car he had. By the time I expressed my differences, the salesman came back and Willie started to argue with me in front of the salesman. He told me that he was not going to put all that money into repairing a car when he could buy a new one. He said that I needed to stop trying to rule over him and that I had no place telling him what to do.

The salesman saw that I had no power in the whole car deal so they went ahead with the transaction. To his surprise, the new car started to have problems about six months later and Willie ended up trading that car in too. Fortunately, he ended up with a better looking car. I came home one evening, and saw another car in the garage thinking it was another loaner car, and that the other one was being checked. When I saw that the car tag was his previous tag from the other car, I just said Lord have mercy on my husband. I felt that another salesman had sweet-talked him and he jumped for that one also. He made sure when he traded the white car that I wasn't around, and he didn't tell me anything. The reason for that was he did not want my input on it.

I planned a Father's Day outing for Willie in downtown Atlanta that Sunday evening. My plans fell through because Willie ended up getting so angry with Jamar for not taking the trashcan out to the garage as soon as he told him to. Jamar was planning on doing that when he was finished doing his homework so he wouldn't have that to do when we got back home that night. Willie got so angry to the point he took his belt off to whip Jamar. Jamar ran from the table and went upstairs and hid under the guest bedroom bed to escape that whipping knowing that his dad could not get down on the floor to whip him under the bed. When Willie was going upstairs after Jamar, I yelled upstairs and told Jamar to hide somewhere out his dad way.

We ended up not going anywhere. Jamar stayed under the bed that night because he didn't want his dad to find him. Jamar was too afraid to finish his homework no matter how much I pleaded with him to come out from under the bed. He'd prefer to get a zero on his homework than to get a whipping. I monitored Willie movements when he went downstairs or go out in the garage so that Jamar could come out and use the restroom or something. The next morning after the incident, I told Jamar to get dressed and get to the car quickly. He ate his breakfast in the car on the way to school. As I was getting ready to back the car out of the garage, Willie came out into the garage. I said good morning and told him to have a good day. Willie did not respond to me.

When we got back home that evening, Willie didn't bring up the incident. Upset, I shared with Willie that he'd terrified Jamar and caused him not to finish his homework and that he spoiled Father's Day. After I said that, Willie starting slamming doors and saying that he was going to pack some clothes and leave for a few days. He said that we could have the whole house to ourselves. The next day he left. I was relieved that he'd given us a little break. I prayed that he'd be okay wherever he went. Later that evening, I was relieved to know that he was at my Cousin Debra's house in Jacksonville, Florida. I could not believe that he took the chance to drive that distance by himself.

Willie returned home the Thursday after Father's day weekend. Regardless of how he had acted on Father's Day, we still presented him with the gifts we bought for him. He seemed to have appreciated them.

We took Willie out for a Father's Day Dinner later that evening. It was sad that he would get so furious toward us, the ones that he held closest to his heart. It was also sad to know that he couldn't even remember what he was so angry about sometimes. For some reason, I would always let forgiveness flow through my heart for him and cherish him anyway.

Chapter 10

We planned a trip to Las Vegas for a few days. We went to drop Jamar off at our friend Faith's house. While I was standing on her porch giving her some last minute instructions about Jamar, Willie started to get irritated and impatient. He said that if I didn't hurry up so we could leave and get to the airport in time, he was going to take off and leave me right there.

I told him that I was coming. When I went into her house to kiss Jamar goodbye, I heard Faith say Melvina, your husband took off and left you. I ran to the door and saw that it was true. I was so embarrassed because Faith didn't know about Willie's condition and actions. There I was again, trying to explain the reason for Willie's actions. I was so upset with him that I started crying. Jamar even felt sorry for me.

As I sat in the living room contemplating what to do for at least fifteen minutes, Faith started jumping up and down. She was by her front door and said with relief that Willie was back. I hurried out the door and to the car. I was relieved as well, but I was angry when I got in the car. Willie told me that he wanted to show me that he would leave me at any given time. If we had missed the plane, I knew for sure that he would have blamed me. It was a good thing that we had ample time.

When we arrived at Atlanta's Hartsfield Airport, everything went smoothly. The wheel chair assistant was there waiting on Willie to wheel him to the departure gate. I'd requested that there be a wheel chair assistant waiting at the Las Vegas airport when we arrived. When we got on the plane and were settled, I began to panic. Even though I've flown on many planes before, I always got a little nervous thinking about what could go wrong. As I was fidgeting and mumbling about it, Willie got fed up and said that I was acting like I'd never been on a plane before. He then told me as loudly as he could to shut up and move to another seat.

I told him that I just couldn't go and sit somewhere else. The plane was full anyway. He then told me that the next time a flight attendant comes, he was going to ask her to move me. I just sat straight and stayed quiet so that he wouldn't embarrass me any further. I hoped he would forget. But he didn't. As soon as the flight attendant walked by, he stopped her and told her that he wanted her to move me because I was getting on his nerves. She turned to him and said that the plane was at capacity and that everything would be okay. She added that lots of people are fearful of flying, even she was and she had been a flight attendant for many years. He then blurted out that the next time we planned a trip, we were going to take separate flights and just meet up at the airport.

When we arrived at the Las Vegas airport things took a turn. When we got off the plane and went into the airport waiting area, there were no wheel chairs or wheel chair assistants to wheel him down to the baggage claim area. I was a little disappointed and I saw the anger on Willie's

116

face. It was really busy in there and everyone looked like they were moving in the fast lane.

I grabbed the nearest staff and asked them about the wheelchairs and they said that they had none available but that they'd be back to help. I took one look at Willie as he was fussing. He started walking with his cane, and I told him that it was too far for him to walk. He stopped and hit the floor several times with his cane demanding me to stop dictating to him what he couldn't do and what he could do. He told me if I said one more word, then he would have his plane ticket changed and get on the first flight home. He said that I could stay if I wanted too. I walked away from him to find him a wheelchair. It wasn't long before I saw an abandoned one.

When Willie saw me coming with it, he griped about getting in it. He told me that he didn't need my help. As soon as Willie got in the wheelchair, I saw an assistant coming in our direction with an empty wheelchair to assist Willie. A little while later, as I waited for the luggage, I saw Willie having a conversation with another attendant, laughing and making jokes. At that moment, I just thanked the Lord and asked Him to please let Willie stay in that pleasant mood throughout our trip. Thankfully, Willie did very well and we had a lovely time taking part in several activities. I knew what not to do on our flight back home.

A few days later, I got a call from my brother Eugene stating that my mom's condition had gotten worse. He told me that she had to be hospitalized and was not coherent. It was puzzling to me, because I'd just talked to her on the phone the day before, after our trip from Vegas, and she was doing okay. I knew she'd pull through because she'd been on dialysis for approximately three years and we were used to her going in and out of the hospital due to complications. Her physician said that she had congestive heart failure due to the malfunctioning of her kidneys. This time she was in the hospital for a bacterial infection.

In the beginning of the third week while she was still in the hospital, my mother had begun to feel a little better, but something in my spirit told me to go and visit her for the weekend. I took off that Friday with Jamar and went to see her. As soon as I reached Charleston, SC., we went to the hospital. When we got to her room she was a little coherent, but in so much pain that she could hardly talk.

About a month after my mother entered the hospital, she was discharged from the hospital. She passed away later that same day. When I got the call that she had died, I could not believe it. I dropped the phone down on the bed. I became very numb. I was so shocked and in denial that I couldn't even cry right then. I didn't even know how to tell Willie and Jamar. When I did, I burst into tears and Willie tried to comfort me as much as his nerves allowed him too.

Attending my mother's funeral was one of the weakest days of my life. Before leaving to travel back home to Georgia after her funeral that evening, we all stopped at a gas station to fill up, including Lee and his wife Judy and also a sister-n-law of mine (Phyllis). They all were driving separate cars. After we all filled up our cars with gas, Lee simply asked Willie which route we were going to take to go back to Georgia. He wanted to know if we were going I-26 to I-20, or taking another route that we all knew about which was a little shorter. Willie didn't answer him. I asked why he didn't answer the question. Willie then lashed out saying that he didn't need any of us niggers to tell him how to travel.

Everyone was just shocked and I was yet again, embarrassed. I got out of the car and stood in between Lee's car and our car while I was trying to reason with Willie and make him understand that no one was trying to tell him which way to travel back. Lee only wanted to know which direction so we could all travel together. Willie jumped into the car and sped off with Jamar inside. I got in the car with Phyllis and we followed behind Lee's car.

Later on, on the interstate, we caught up with Willie. When we got up near him in the passing lane, I told Phyllis to blow her car horn at him so we could try and get his attention. I wanted to see if he would roll down his windows so I could tell him to stop so I could help him drive. Willie did not even look our way. Jamar saw us trying to get his dad attention, but I figured he didn't say anything to Willie because he was afraid. Again, I had to try and explain to Phyllis the reasons for Willie's actions. She really didn't understand what I was explaining to her. I felt really bad when she asked me what was wrong with him acting like that and calling people names. She did not like that, neither did Lee and Judy. I told Phyllis to please hurry up and get me home before Willie got home, because if he gets home before I do, he might lock me out. I was very happy that I did get home before he did. When I heard the garage door open as he was driving in, I hurried and went upstairs to get out of his way. The first thing that Willie did when he walked in the house was to yell my name demanding me to come downstairs right away. I just said Lord, please have mercy on me and why was Willie treating me this way when I just buried my mother. When I got down the stairs, I pleaded with him to not fuss with me because I didn't do anything wrong. I asked that he could at least take it under consideration that I would be grieving. He told me that he didn't care about any grieving and he didn't want to know how I felt. He said that I had had better not pull that stunt on him ever again, making people think that he did not know the way back home or how to travel alone. He also stated that he did not need anyone to follow him nor did he need to follow anyone like he was a child that had to be led.

Jamar asked me why his dad acted the way he did even though no one did anything. I told him that I didn't know what was going through his father's mind. Then Jamar said that he didn't want to ride in the same car with his dad and me because there was always an argument. I thought about my husband that night. It was amazing how sometimes I'd get compliments on how great and sweet my husband was from some people. Those are the ones that have never seen his other side. They just didn't know what went on behind closed doors. If only they knew.

In October, Lee called and told me that he wanted to take me out for my birthday as a mother and son outing. He said that he probably knew that Willie and Jamar were going to take me out one day that weekend. So, it was my choice as to which day I wanted him to take me out. I told him that I had to check with Willie first.

When I brought it up to Willie, he acted as if he was jealous of Lee taking me out and said that I could do whatever the hell I wanted to. Since Willie acted that way, I ended up having to lie to Lee, telling him that Willie had plans for me both days that weekend. My cousin Henry called the house to see if we were going to be home later on in the evening, if so, he was going to stop by. I told him that Willie and Jamar were going to take me out to a restaurant to celebrate my birthday later on. I asked him if he wanted to join us and he said yes.

I told Willie after I hung up the phone with Henry. Willie was lying down on the couch in the living room watching television. When I told him that Henry was coming over to go with us, he became really upset and said, every time we plan to go somewhere, I always had to invite a crowd. I didn't think that he would have gotten upset about me inviting Henry. Willie told me earlier in the afternoon that we were leaving around 5:00 o'clock and asked me what time did I tell Henry. I told him 5:00 o'clock. Willie said that if Henry wasn't at the house by that time, he'd leave us and go eat by himself.

It was close to 5:30 when Willie gotten fed up and went to the garage to get in his car to leave. Fortunately Henry drove up as Willie was backing out of the garage. When we all got in the car with Willie, he told us that he was tired of waiting for slow behind people. Henry just shook his head in disbelief. As we were looking over our menus, I asked Willie if he wanted me to help him read the menu since the lighting was so dim. He blurted out that he didn't need anyone to help him because he wasn't a child. He said that he had the authority to order his own darn blasted food. For the rest of the night I was on pins and needles trying not to say a word to him.

The waiter asked for our orders. Jamar, was sitting next to Willie, noticed that his dad was having a hard time reading the small print, and asked if he could help. Willie told him to shut up and leave him alone. Willie really embarrassed us all. When we were getting ready to leave the restaurant, Willie and Jamar went to the restroom. Henry told me that he did not know if he wanted to go anywhere with us together again, because Willie sure knew how to mess up things. I tried to explain that he was suffering from PTSD and the symptoms made him capable of acting out like that at times. Henry seemed to think that Willie was just being mean and ugly.

On our way home from the restaurant, Henry asked Willie to stop at his friend Billy's house so that he could retrieve a house key, just in case Billy decided to leave before he got back. When we arrived, Henry went inside the house. After a few minutes, Willie started to complain that Henry was taking too long and that he was going to leave him. He added that Henry could get back to our house the best way he could to pick up his car. I asked Willie to give Henry another minute. Willie responded by saying he did not like waiting on someone who was just running his mouth. I hoped that Henry would come out soon, because I knew Willie would leave him. A few more minutes passed and Willie started his ignition. I pleaded with him not to leave. I told him that I would go in and get Henry. He told me that I'd better hurry up or he'd leave me too.

I ran up to Billy's door to tell Henry Willie was ready. Billy came out on the porch, stretched out his arms and gave me a friendly hug stating that he hadn't seen me in a very long time. He waved his hand at Willie saying hello to him as he was sitting in the car. Of course, Willie did not speak back to him or wave his hand. Henry didn't tarry when we got back to the house. He quickly got out of the car and immediately got into his car and left. I guess he'd had enough of Willie for the evening. As soon as he left, Willie started to argue. He told me that he didn't like the idea of me letting Billy hug me and me hugging him back. Willie said that my purpose for going up to Billy's door was to get Henry out of there, not to hug anyone.

Willie was really upset with me to the point he did not want to sleep in the bed with me. Later on that night, he gathered two pillows from our bedroom and went downstairs to sleep on the floor. Before I went to bed, I came downstairs to tell Willie goodnight, but I saw that he was already sound asleep. I was startled when I saw his briefcase that he usually kept his gun in, in the trunk of the car, lying down by his side. I was even more startled to realize that he had the gun lying on the floor near his head with his hand on it. My heart then skipped a beat. I was terrified. At that moment, I couldn't think about what to do. I didn't know what was going on in his mind or what he'd planned to do. My mind was running a mile a minute. I started to call the police, but I decided against it because I thought he'd pull the trigger on himself if the police had come up to the door; better yet, he might have killed all of us.

I eased back upstairs to get my mace container and to wake up Jamar to let him know what was going on with his father. I told him to get up and put some clothes on so we could escape out of the house. I was going to get a hotel room. I told him that his father had his gun out, and I didn't want to chance us getting hurt. Jamar sleepily said that he didn't want to go anywhere and that he didn't think his father would do anything to hurt us. He said that his father had the gun for protection. I couldn't convince Jamar that it was unusual for his dad to have a gun near his head with his hand on it. I didn't want Willie to hear us either. Jamar went back in his bed and thought nothing of it. I couldn't let that go just like that.

I sat high up on the stair steps so Willie couldn't see me. I kept my eyes on him. If I had seen Willie coming toward the stair steps to come up with the gun in his hand, I would have certainly sprayed him with the mace and called the police. I could only think, if he did, he was coming to harm us, not knowing what frame of mind he was in. He woke up twice to go to the garage to smoke cigarettes; he didn't see me on the stairs. The first time he went, he had the gun in his hand. I was hoping that he did not go out to the garage to kill himself. Willie came back in and laid back down on the floor with the gun placed at the top of his head again.

The second time he went out in the garage, he left the gun on the floor. At that moment, I decided to go to the living room and move the gun. I was afraid to touch it thinking it may have gone off. I took a chance and moved it before he came back in the house. I quickly locked it in the briefcase and kept the key. I went to the garage where he was. I asked him what was going on and why he brought the gun in the house and placed it at his head. He said that he had it there to protect him and his family. He said he felt that someone was coming to harm all of us or steal his family away from him. I asked Willie what made him feel like that and who did he think was coming to do such a thing? He suggested that I figure it out. If I couldn't he said, then I should think back on that man that I was hugging up on and grinning with earlier that evening. Willie was jealous and was talking about Billy. I couldn't believe that he was thinking like that. I prayed for our safety. It seemed to me like Willie was really psyching out.

When we came back into the house, Willie went back in the living room to lie back on the floor. He discovered that I had moved his gun and locked it up in the briefcase. He yelled at me demanding that I give back his key. I told him I was afraid that he'd snap and shoot us all. Willie became more irate and in a rage about me moving his gun. Jamar woke up from the commotion and came downstairs to see what was going on. I told him what I did. Jamar wanted me to give the key back to his father, but I said no. Jamar didn't understand his father's psychological problems like I did. There was no way I was giving that key back to him. If I did, I stood the chance of him using it while he was angry.

The next morning after I dropped Jamar off to school, I went on to work. When I arrived, my normal parking space was occupied. I parked in the back of the building near a tree. Willie called me three hours later telling me that he'd just come from the parking lot at my job and he didn't see my car. He asked me which one of my men I had laid up with that morning. I told him about my parking situation and also added that he could come back up there to see where I was parked. He said that I was lying and that I better have his key to his briefcase when I get home from work. I was determined not to give him that key anytime soon no matter how much he fussed.

About three weeks later after that ordeal, Willie decided to go and visit his friend Ronald in Huntsville, Alabama for the weekend. He demanded that I give him his key so that he could take his gun with him on the highway for protection. I went ahead and gave it to him since he was getting ready to travel by himself. When I gave him the key, he told me that I had better not touch his briefcase key and gun ever again. I really didn't want him to have it for anything. The night before Willie left, he put the gun up on the dresser out of the briefcase and told me that he was showing me that he could put his gun anywhere in the house when he wanted too. That was another night that I stayed up watching every movement Willie made and being afraid.

Jamar wanted his best friend to come over and spend the weekend with us. He would usually ask me for everything, knowing that his dad would usually answer no. I told him yes after I consulted with Daniel's parents. I figured that would be a good time to have him over so they could have fun without Willie being home griping about everything. Daniel came home with us that Friday evening when I picked them up from school. In the past, Daniel used to come every so often and spend the weekends with us because of his parents' business travel.

When Willie returned home, he picked Jamar up from school. Jamar told him that Daniel had spent the weekend with us. Willie couldn't wait to get home to fuss at me. I told him that I didn't think it was a big deal. He asked me who brought Daniel over. I shared that he came with us after school. Willie then asked me, who came to pick him up that Sunday evening? I told him that his father did. Willie really got upset saying that he didn't want any men on his property when he's not home. I told him that Daniel's father did not come in the house. Willie said that he didn't care. He added that I should pack my clothes to go live with them since I wanted Daniel's father so badly.

Later on that night, Willie began looking around the house as if he were trying to find someone lurking behind the furniture or in the closets. I was hoping that this incident wouldn't make him bring his gun back in the house. Willie was so paranoid that anytime the phone rang he'd swear up and down that I was talking to another man, just to make sure; he'd pick up the phone sometimes and listen in on my conversations.

One day, I decided to go without Willie to the VA hospital to see his mental health physician, Dr. Dent. I told her about the gun incident. She asked me why I was still there putting my child and myself in danger like that. I responded that I really didn't have a reason other than I loved him and that I wanted to keep my family together. Dr. Dent said that I'd better give that a second thought. She said that I should start thinking about a "getaway" plan because I couldn't fix what was wrong with him. She added that it appeared to her as though I was trying to fix my husband's problems and in the mean time was putting our lives in jeopardy.

She reminded me that Willie was suffering from a severe case of PTSD and there was no cure for it, but the symptoms could be managed. She suggested I get rid of the gun and to go to the police station with a statement drawn

127

up by her of his mental status. The next time Willie goes to purchase a gun, hopefully they would do a thorough background check that would prevent him from obtaining one. I didn't go through with it because I was truly afraid. I knew if I had gotten rid of it he would have been angrier.

A few weeks later Willie and I went to see Dr. Dent together. I wanted to see if he would bring up the gun incident. He didn't. Dr. Dent asked Willie how he was feeling. Willie said that he felt lifeless. She asked him if he'd had any suicidal thoughts. Willie hung his head down and said that he could not answer that question. When he did not answer that question, I realized that he was suicidal. She asked had he been taking his meds and he didn't answer. She told him that he needed to get a grip on his life and asked him if he loved his family. He said that he did, but that he didn't feel loved. Dr. Dent replied to him that he should feel loved and that he was very blessed to have a wife that would stick with him. She said that many relationships of this caliber didn't last. She admitted that she didn't think she could have lasted in a relationship like ours or her other patients, from what she'd heard occurring with some of the veterans and their families dealing with the mental challenges.

Willie responded that he didn't feel blessed by anyone except God. Dr. Dent saw that she wasn't getting through to him, so she just prescribed some different meds and scheduled him for anger management classes. Before we left her office, she made sure to reiterate that he was indeed blessed to have me in his life. As soon as we returned home, Willie threw all of the medication bags up in the medicine cabinet. He stated that he wasn't ready to be changing meds and I had better not say anything about it.

I went to my own doctor for a check-up, I ended up telling her about the gun incident and she too asked why I stayed in a relationship like that. She told me that the relationship was very unhealthy and sadly, our young son was being dragged through it as well. I decided to ask Willie if we could speak with a marriage counselor at church and to attend prayer sessions. He said that we did not need to do that. He added that if I did decide to go, I better not tell the counselor anything about him because if I did, he would bust my behind wide open and tell them to come and clean me up from the floor. I knew I had better not press the issue any longer. I was somewhat relieved when he started keeping the gun in the car trunk, but I was still paranoid about him having it.

Lee and his wife invited us to my grandson's, John, christening at their church. The ceremony included recognition of family. The person, who was calling the names to come up, somehow neglected to call our names. All of a sudden, Willie got up and said to me how disrespectful that was and that we wasted our time going there just to get embarrassed. Some people looked back at him. Willie got up and stormed out of the door. I knew he had left Jamar and me there. A friend of theirs did the calling of names and their titles.

After the service, Lee asked what happened to Willie. I told him that I didn't want to tell him right then. One of Lee and Judy's friends gave us a ride home, because he was the only one who had room in his car. I didn't tell Lee's friend anything about why Willie acted like that and left us. When we got home and walked inside, Willie let me have it. He told me not to ever take him anywhere again to have him embarrassed like that. He asked, who were we supposed to be, nobody? Willie said a blind man could have seen through that. He said never again was that going to happen. He said that we would have been better off going to our own church that Sunday. It was a very long time before I told Lee about that situation. He was shocked. Lee said that he did not realize that they had left our names out. Lee also said that we should have just gotten up anyway; knowing us, we were not going to do that unless our names were called.

A week before the Christmas Holiday, Jamar was in a school play at our church. After the play, I was standing there talking to a couple of his teachers when Willie said to me that I had better hurry up because he was ready to go. Jamar had gone out with him. After I got through speaking with the teachers, for about ten minutes, I went on outside to go to the car and detected that the car was not outside. Willie was gone. I stood there in shock as it rained. I tried calling him to see where he had gone but his phone was off. I began to panic, thinking he had left me wondering how I was going to get home. After about twenty minutes he showed up. I was so mad at him. I blessed him out really bad. Jamar was looking at me and he put his finger up to his lips trying to tell me to be quiet before I upset his father. Willie said that he would do it again. He said the only reason he came back for me was because Jamar was in the back seat crying and worrying about something happening to me. Willie said he was showing me that he meant business.

130

Chapter 11

Willie decided suddenly one day that he needed to go back to see his friend Ronald in Huntsville Alabama that upcoming Friday. I asked him if something was wrong. He said no. He said that he needed to go and check on something. He wouldn't tell me why he was going. At least he wasn't upset this time before leaving. I told him that he really needed to stay off that highway by himself. When Willie returned home on Sunday evening, I was in the kitchen cooking dinner. He called the house from his cell phone to tell us to open the garage door because it was locked and to have Jamar come out side for a minute.

Jamar went outside to see what his father wanted. I got curious after about twenty minutes and went out in the garage to look outside to see what they were doing for so long. When I went outside, I saw Willie standing against the car looking through some papers and he had a pet carrier at his side. I became curious to know why he had it. When Jamar turned around to face me, he had a small puppy in his hands. I started fussing with Willie so much to the point I suddenly experienced a sharp pain in my chest making me feel like I was having a heart attack or something. It hurt so bad that tears were trickling down my face. Willie knew I did not want any pets because I did not like them and I was afraid they might bite or scratch. In addition, I felt the pet was going to be a lot of work. I had my hands filled already with Willie and Jamar. Willie said he had gotten tired of Jamar asking for a dog every year at Christmas or for his birthday. When Jamar first asked for a dog, I said no and told him why. He tried to convince me that the pet would not harm me. My answers were always no and I meant that. I was yet again, defeated and just outdone. Later that night, Jamar brought the puppy over to me while I was sitting at the kitchen table for me to feel him. I said no.

After Jamar saw that I had calmed down a little, he asked me would I help him to name his pet. Jamar was just trying so hard to make me like the dog. I started spitting out some names to make Jamar happy. Jamar decided that he liked the name Pappy. Pappy didn't come near me too much. He must have sensed that I didn't like dogs.

One day, Willie took Pappy to get his vaccination shots while I was at work and Jamar was at school. When Jamar and I came in that evening, Willie was on the couch sleeping. Jamar went upstairs to take a shower. I stayed downstairs a few minutes before I went up to retrieve the voice messages of the phone. While I was sitting there, I heard an unusual faint growling noise. I went to the living room first to see if it was Willie. When I found out that it wasn't him, I went to look in Pappy's cage to see if that was Pappy growling. When I looked in there, I saw that he was swollen up about three times his normal size until I couldn't see his face. I yelled out to Willie telling him to hurry and get Pappy to the hospital.

I told Willie that Pappy must've had an allergic reaction to his shots earlier that day. I was very paranoid and worried about him. I hoped and prayed that nothing bad would happen to him. When Jamar came down, I told him what had happened to Pappy and that his father took him to the hospital. Jamar became very worried, crying and carrying on until I had to take him to the hospital where Pappy and his dad were. I tried to comfort him on the way, telling him that a pet is just like a human being. They do get sick at times and have to go to the doctor or to the hospital. It was just truly a blessing from God that I had lingered downstairs for a little bit in order to detect that Pappy was in danger. If I had gone on upstairs when I first came in, we probably would found Pappy later on dead. If that had happened, I didn't know how we all would have taken that, especially Jamar. I felt so sorry for him. The pet hospital did keep Pappy over night to observe and monitor him because he did have an allergic reaction to one of his vaccination shots.

Since that incident, even though I did not want Pappy around, I started paying more attention to him. After Pappy started detecting that I was paying attention to him, he became more attached to me than to Willie and Jamar. When Pappy needed to go outside or wanted to eat or something, he would bypass them and come up to me, showings me signs of what he wanted. He always followed me around. I became the one taking care of Pappy more so than Willie or Jamar.

Another Valentine's Day came. I received a gift basket from an anonymous person while at work. I wondered all day about whom it could've come from. I was certainly afraid to call and ask Willie, because if it weren't from him, then it would've been the biggest mess. I really couldn't think of any one else who would send me flowers. I didn't take the chance of asking. I had better sense than that. I decided to leave the basket at work instead of taking it home. I dropped by the store to get a dozen roses and a card for Willie. When I got home, Willie was in the living room with a big smile on his face. He was thankful for what I'd brought home for him.

All of a sudden, Willie attitude changed and he started to snap at everything I said to him. I asked him what was wrong. He said that I could've at least showed him some appreciation for the basket that he sent me at work and that he was upset that I did not bring it home. I told him that I didn't mention anything about it or bring it home because I'd had such a hectic day. I forgot and left them on my desk. I told him thanks and that the basket was beautiful and I would definitely bring it home the next day.

Chapter 12

On Easter Sunday, our Bishop called for an altar prayer for those who wanted to be delivered from all bad habits. He particularly wanted the cigarette smokers to come to the altar and place their cigarettes on it. The Bishop also said that for those who left their cigarettes in the car or something, he still wanted them to come down and touch the altar with their hands. Jamar and I looked at Willie and urged him to go. His excuse was that he was not about to walk through the large crowd to touch no altar and that God would take care of him.

When the service was over, Jamar and I got into the car first. Jamar took Willie's cigarettes and hid them. Jamar whispered to me as Willie got in the car and told me not to tell on him. The first thing Willie did was look for his cigarettes. When he couldn't find them, he acted as if he was having a nicotine attack. He asked us where we put them because he knew we had them. We didn't say anything. Willie didn't waste any time, he stopped at the first store he saw and bought more. I told him that he was being ridiculous for not going to the altar to get free from his addiction. Willie just smiled.

A couple weeks later, there was a men's conference at our church that started on a Wednesday evening and ended on Saturday. When he came home that Wednesday night, he complained about numbness and tingling in his left arm, hand and foot. I told him that those were possible signs of a stroke. I asked him to let me take his blood pressure. He refused afraid, that it might have been high. After pleading with him for a while, he finally agreed. I took it and it was much higher than his normal readings. I suggested taking him to the hospital. Willie fought against me and said that there was no way that he was going and sit up in a hospital all night. I said I was going to call the 911 for EMS, to see if they would convince him to go. He told me that he was all right and for me not to call anyone. I stayed up all night monitoring Willie.

On Thursday morning, Willie seemed to be doing okay without any symptoms. I tried to get him to go and see his physician to check him out because of the symptoms he'd experienced the night before. Willie said that he was feeling all right and that he was going back to attend the conference sessions at church. When Willie returned home Thursday night, he had those same symptoms. On Friday morning he went back to the church conference. I suggested again that instead of him going to the conference, he should go to the doctor's office.

While Willie was at the conference Friday morning, one of the preachers happened to be talking about men and their health. The preacher made a statement that men don't go to the doctor until it's too late. As soon as the preacher said that, Willie left the conference and called me telling me what was said and to call the doctors office. I told him to just go as a walk-in patient and that I will get off work and meet him. Willie arrived before I did. He called me on the cell phone saying not to come because the office was getting ready to close and that the doctor had already left. The office closed at noon.

He told me that one of the receptionists who was still there told Willie to go on over to the hospital. He said he told the receptionist that she was telling him the same thing that I told him. His told her that he didn't want to go because he didn't want to be there hours on end waiting, and he definitely didn't want to be admitted. I encouraged him to go and said I would just meet him at the hospital. He hung up on me. I was hoping that he had changed his mind and had gone on to the hospital. I went on over to the hospital waiting around to see if he was going to show up. When I did not see him after an hour, I called him several times, but he did not answer his cell phone. I began to worry about where he could be. I called the house, he did not answer. I decided to go home. When I got home, Willie was lying down watching TV.

I told him that it appeared to me like he was playing around with his health when he could have been at the hospital being checked out rather than lying down at home watching TV. He asked me to just leave him alone. I prayed that God would make him go and get check.

He suffered with those symptoms the whole weekend. I told him Sunday night that I was taking him to his doctors' office if I had to drag him there on Monday morning. Fortunately, he gave into me and said that he would go. I took him. Blood work was done on him and also a head scan (x-ray of the head) was ordered to see whether or not he had a stroke. All the test results showed that he'd had a mild stroke. The only thing that needed to be done to him was for him to take the meds that the doctor prescribed and an aspirin daily to help prevent blood clots. He also needed to get some therapy done on that entire left side to strengthen it. The doctor stressed the fact that he must do what he was told or he could risk losing the use of that side of his body. His doctor asked me to call back the next day to get the information on where Willie needed to go for his therapy.

When I told Willie, he lashed out at me and told me that he was not going and that he did not have time for that therapy mess. I asked him what mess and what else he had to do. I stressed to him that going to therapy would benefit him much better than him lying around at home, stressing about everything and smoking cigarettes. I thanked God that the mild stroke did not get him all the way down. From time to time, he would complain about the tingling, weakness and numbness.

One Saturday afternoon, Willie asked me if I would like to ride with him down to South GA to visit another one of his former Vietnam veteran buddies, Fred and his Wife Marlene. I agreed to go. When we got near to where they lived, I said to him to please not stay to long, because we needed to get back before it got late and that I needed to stop to the supermarket. We also needed to get situated for church Sunday morning. When I said that Willie totally exploded, yelling that he did not need me to tell him when to leave and that I should have stayed home. He said that he was going to stop at the first service station that he saw and put me out. Willie stopped and told me to get out. Jamar pleaded with his dad not to do that to me because I'd done nothing wrong. I didn't get out. I kept my mouth

138

closed and I told Jamar to do the same thing. When Willie saw that I was not getting out the car, he got out of the car crying, stating that no one loved him and it seemed like everyone is trying to dictate his life by not letting him be himself. My heart hurt for him.

Jamar asked me what was wrong with his dad and why was he crying. I responded that I did not know why. Jamar said that if I had gotten out of the car, he would have also. He was definitely not staying with his dad. Willie proceeded to open the car trunk. I got worried and watched him to see if he was going to get his gun to shoot us, or better yet, shoot himself. He pulled out a pack of cigarettes. I was relieved. Some people drove up in a car and parked near us. Willie started fussing with me again as they were looking at us. I guess they were trying to figure out what was going on with us. Willie happened to see them looking and asked them what were they looking at and asked them if they wanted piece of the deal too. I was hoping that they did not say anything back to him.   I looked over at the people and put my finger across my lips, signaling them not to say anything to Willie. They didn't. They went ahead and left. Willie finally calmed down a little bit and we went on to Fred and Marlene's house. When we drove into their driveway, I got out first and was able to tell Fred a little bit of our ordeal and the reason why we were just getting there. I asked him to please try and talk to Willie without him not knowing what I had just told him. I told him that I didn't think Willie was going to change because of him just talking with him. Fred said that he would try the best he could. He also stated that he felt that Willie was not taking his meds like he should.

Fred told me not to worry. Fred shared with him that he looked stressed out and asked him if he is taking all of his medications? Willie didn't comment on that. He got on another subject. After we finished eating dinner, Fred took Jamar around to the den so he could play around on the computer. While we were in conversation, Fred pulled out his meds and laid them on the table. He told Willie that the meds especially for PTSD and depression were keeping him sane and helping him to have a better life. He told Willie that he should do the same and to never slack up on his meds when he felt like it no matter how it made him feel. Willie said to Fred that everyone's system is different and that many can handle more than some.

When we got back home Willie heeded Fred's advice for a little while, but then he slacked up again. At times, I could not tell Willie anything. I had written several love letters to Willie in the past expressing my feelings toward him. He read one of them, saw the others I had written and tore them up. He had no comments about it. He was angry with me for writing him the letters. He told me if I had something to tell him, just say it. I shared that he was not going to listen.

One weekend, we went down to Charleston, SC to attend a function and were forced by Willie's demanding rage to leave our hotel room early in the morning, around 3:30am. We had to come back home the same night of the function. I had gone down to the front desk to get someone to come to our room to see if they could talk with Willie and try to calm him down. A couple security guards came and tried, but made no headway with Willie. We did not have the opportunity to get any sleep. Willie got upset

140

because I had gone over to talk with some people that I knew from the area where I grew up. They were sitting at a table near where we were getting the food. Willie did not give me a chance to introduce him because he had gotten an attitude and did not want to meet them. Two of them were males. Willie accused me of liking them.

After a couple of hours of traveling, Willie said that he was hungry. I replied that the only restaurant that was open was Waffle House. I told him that the next one that I saw, I would stop. About ten miles down the highway, I saw the sign. When I got near the exit to get off, Willie thought that I was going to pass it by and all of a sudden he reached over and pulled the keys out of the ignition while I was driving and the car stopped suddenly in the middle of the exit ramp. Jamar started screaming, thinking another vehicle may have hit us in the back. It was truly a blessing there weren't any vehicles coming up closely behind us. I called the police.

The officer arrived and told Willie the danger that we all could have endured and for him to never do something like that again. Of course, he got more upset because I called the police. About a half hour later in our trip, Willie said that he needed me to stop at a service station to get a bottle of water. When I drove up to the service station and parked the car, I asked Jamar to go inside and get the water for his dad and asked if he had the money. Before Jamar could answer, Willie took his right fist and hit me on my chin. It really hurt and became a little swollen. Jamar asked his dad, why he hit me.

Willie told the both of us to shut up because I acted as if he didn't have any money. I was hurting so badly, to the point that I went into the store to get some Tylenol or Aleve, holding my chin and crying. The clerk asked me if I was okay or not. I shared with her what had happened and the pain I was in. She asked me if I needed her to call the police and the paramedics. I tearfully said yes.

When the policeman came, I told him what happened. He talked to Willie and said that he could take him in his custody for being combative if I wanted to press charges. I said that I was not going to press charges because my husband was a very ill man and I then pulled out a copy of his medications list that I usually keep in my purse. When the officer saw the list, it almost took his breath away. After I explained some of what was actually going on with Willie, the officer said that he felt very sorry for Willie. When the paramedic arrived, I had them to take Willie to the hospital to get checked out instead of me. I told them that I would go to the hospital if I needed to when I got back home.

The hospital staff checked Willie out and released him a few hours later and told him that he needed to follow up with his physicians immediately when he returned home. He was stressing too much. As we continued to travel, Willie tried opening the car door so he could fall out on the highway. Jamar and I had a very tough time trying to keep the door locked so Willie wouldn't open it. I asked Willie if he wanted to fall out of a moving car and get killed. He said yes; and that he did not care if he died like that.

I often sighed when I heard the garage going up knowing Willie was coming home. Jamar took notice of me doing that and asked why I sighed when I heard his daddy driving in the garage. I was shocked when he asked me

142

that. I said it was because I didn't know what kind of mood his dad would be in when he comes in. I tried very hard to be prepared for Willie's mood swings/split personalities.

Things got so horrible to the point I called Fred and asked what he thought about me crushing Willie's meds up and placing them in his food. I told Fred that I felt very bad asking him a question like that. He said that if that was the only way that I could get the meds in his system properly, then I should do it. Fred stressed the fact to me that it wasn't anything illegal about it. Those meds were specifically prescribed from his mental health physician for him to take and that I must realize that I have to treat Willie just like taking care of a child that needed their medications which had to be administered by their parents or other adults. I started to call Willie's mental health physician and ask the same question that I asked Fred about me crushing Willie's meds. I did not call and I also decided not to take Fred's advice. My conscious, along with me being afraid did not allow me to do that even though it seemed like it was something good to do. I just couldn't do it.

When Willie did take the meds like he should, it seemed that some days it would keep him calm, but yet, made him feel really bad, down and out at the same time. Some days it was like he did not have any in his system and was sitting on a time bomb ready to explode. Some of the meds made him sleep a lot and feel very sluggish. He could hardly function properly. I was afraid, thinking if I did go ahead with putting the meds in his food, he might have gotten into his car putting his life or someone else's life in jeopardy by causing an accident or something. If something

143

like that had happened, I didn't think that I could ever live that one down.

Willie mentioned the symptoms he experienced to his physician and sometimes the physician would change the dosages or the meds. Soon it came to a point that the meds seemed not to work for him as much as I wanted it to, even when he took them on a regular basis. It hurt me so much because I finally realized that I could not fix his problems to make him live a more peaceful and normal life.

Willie never saw things the way we did. We couldn't do anything right. Willie wasn't Willie if he didn't find something wrong to argue about. Most of the times, we couldn't satisfy Willie no matter what.

While Willie was having his medical problems, so was I. I found out that I had a meniscus tear in my right knee that required me to have surgery. I was really nervous and worried about having surgery. I became somewhat depressed wondering how I was going to take care of my family and me. It got to Willie's nerves so badly until he wanted us to take a little mini vacation up to the Tennessee Mountains before I had the surgery. We went and had a relaxing time for once, with no bickering involved, thank the Lord.

I had arranged for a family member to take me to the hospital for my surgery, because I knew that Willie's nerves couldn't handle it. He wouldn't have understood what the surgeon and the other assistants had to say anyway. Willie was all right with that. Jamar stayed home that day from summer camp to be there when I got back to help me. After I got home and got settled a little bit, Willie had the nerve to tell me that he had gotten on Jamar's

144

behind earlier that day about cleaning up his room before
he left out of it. He told me what he was going to do to
Jamar if he didn't do it right away. Shortly after Willie's
statement, he went out to pick up something to eat for us.
While he was gone, I asked Jamar what happened and what
his dad said to him. Jamar told me that he had a horrible
day being home with his dad and started to leave. Willie
told Jamar that he was going to kill him. Willie told Jamar
to clean it up and for Jamar not to say anything back to him
about doing it.

I had just come home from the hospital. I told Jamar
that we would not say anything and just to answer Willie if
he asked a question or something. I apologized to Jamar.

When Willie returned back home with the food, a
cousin and a friend of mine were visiting me. They were
parked in our driveway. Willie got out of his car and came
up to the front door and told them that they had better get
out of his driveway and park on the street. They did not
tarry. They went to move their cars and left. I felt really
bad and embarrassed. Later on that night, I really wanted
to tell Willie about how ugly he acted. I also wanted to ask
him about the threat he made to Jamar, but I was so afraid
of him blowing up at us. I certainly knew that I could not
run on crutches and was not feeling good. I had to do
whatever it took to help keep him from exploding. When
we saw Willie getting started or if he looked angry, we
would completely get out of his way if we could. We dared
not say anything trying to get our points across. We let him
argue on his own until he calmed down.

About a week later, I heard that one of my visitors had
talked really bad about Willie, calling him names. It was

also said that he didn't have to worry about her coming back to our house again and that she would just see me whenever. Eventually, I talked with them about Willie's action, and shared the reason why he acted out like that. They were very pleased with me telling them, in case it happened again, they would understand him better.

There were so many times that I thought about picking up and leaving. Something kept telling me not too and on the other hand, I felt that I would be doing something wrong for leaving and turning my back on Willie, knowing that he needed me. I also felt that God would not forgive me for doing that, even though I felt so guilty for dragging our son through all of the pain.

What I saw happening to Willie from my own point of view was that the PTSD and everything else that came along with it had taken total control of his mind. I often thought that the PTSD seemed as though it was a demon inside of him that was destroying him and was trying to destroy Jamar and me as well. We were the two people that Willie loved, but we were his main targets during his outbursts. It seemed like the older Willie got, the worse his explosive outbursts became; along with the stress he was enduring behind it. I believed that the PTSD was deteriorating Willie's mind.

I was told by the surgeon that I had needed to have another surgery on the same knee because of the problems that I was still having since the first one. The meniscus tissue had torn some more. I shared the news with Willie and I began to cry. He asked me to please don't cry and said that things would be all right.

Willie went with me on my next doctor's appointment, because he said that he needed to talk with the surgeon about my second surgery. Willie said that he needed to let the surgeon know that he had better fix it right this time around. I was sort of worried taking Willie in there. He did tell the surgeon that they needed to do it right, because I was all that he had and he needed his wife. The surgeon told Willie that he could not guarantee that he could fix the problem 100%, but he would try his best to make me feel better. I became deeply depressed after knowing all I had to face with having another surgery. I was very limited in doing certain things after the first surgery and became worse after having another one five months later. I had to be medically treated for my depression.

A few nights later, Willie set up his altar in the living room to pray and meditate in his Bible. After about an hour, he called me from upstairs to come downstairs to where he was. When I came into the living room, Willie told me to get a sheet of paper and a pen or pencil to write down some scriptures from the Bible as he called them out to me. He ended up giving me seventy-three scriptures. After he was finished, I asked him what he was going to do with them. He looked over at me and said that he gave them to me because he wanted me to always study those scriptures. I thought it was pretty strange, but I did not ask him any more questions. He had never done that before.

Chapter 13

One Friday night, after one of Willie's explosive episodes with Jamar and me, Willie's legs became weak and he fell down on the kitchen floor near the refrigerator. Jamar and I asked him what was wrong. Willie told us not to ask him anything. We didn't know what was going on with him because he clouded us with so much fussing. He fussed so much until sweat was just popping out of him making his face shinny and very bright. He managed to get back up and move around like he had been. The next day he went out in his car and was gone for a couple of hours and came back looking like he was all right. Later on that Saturday night, Willie complained about urinating on himself, not being able to get to the bathroom in time.

That Sunday morning, Willie urinated on himself again, twice. I really got concerned because it was unusual for him to urinate on himself, so I called his doctor's office. The on call physician called me back. When I told him what was going on with Willie, he told me that I needed to get him to the hospital immediately because it seemed to him like there was something seriously wrong with Willie. I hung up the phone, paranoid. Willie asked me in a sudden slurred speech pattern what the doctor said. I told him what the doctor said. I assumed right then that he might be having a stroke with those symptoms.

Shortly after arriving at the hospital, Willie was admitted to the intermediate intensive care unit and was put on some blood clotting prevention medications and a MRI of the brain was done. After other brain scans and tests were done, it was determined that Willie had suffered a more serious stroke than the previous one eights months prior. Willie had (cerebral edema), swelling of the brain, but no hemorrhaging (bleeding), thank the Lord. Willie lost the entire use of his left side.

Willie fussed so much that Friday night and Saturday morning over nothing that I didn't see the effects of the stroke on him. I started to wonder if God had allowed this to happen to Willie so he could slow down. At the rate he was going, he could have snapped and seriously done something harmful to all of us. I always prayed that God would heal his mind. I didn't want my husband down and sick like that. I began to think that God also wanted Willie to see just how much Jamar and I really loved him, because he couldn't see it much in his previous frame of mine.

On the other hand, I felt that Willie was victimizing us because of the pain from his past experiences. My depression was haunting me more because I was scheduled to have my second surgery one week after Willie's stroke and was really worried. I went forth with the surgery. I learned that Willie was not going to come home anytime soon according to his neurologist. He would have to be transferred to a nursing/rehabilitation facility after discharge from the hospital because of the paralysis in Willie's entire left side. Other areas were also affected by his stroke. Willie was very concerned and worried about my well being more than his at that time. Everyone who went to the hospital to see him, he would ask them to please go to the house and check on me. He'd rather them come to look after me than him. Even though a lot was going on with us at the same time, I just kept praying, pressing through, depending and leaning on the Lord to raise us back up again.

Willie was transferred to a nursing/rehabilitation center, per his doctor's orders. When his physician told me that, my heart got weak. I never thought the day would come that a loved one of mine would have to be placed in a nursing facility.

After a few days, Willie's speech improved and it was not slurred as much. As time went by, it started to get back to normal. He came down with pneumonia the next day after his transfer from the hospital to the nursing/rehab facility. He got better after a few days. I really tried to show Willie how much I loved him as much as I possibly could.

One day while at the nursing home, I noticed all the veterans had an American flag hanging on their doors. I got one for Willie's door so that everyone would know that my husband served his country proudly also.

All the staff members who assisted Willie thought that he was such a sweet heart and a gentleman. I said to myself, if they only knew what went on in our home behind closed doors. It was a very turbulent journey. Later on, during his stay there, they confided in me that they did detect that Willie was a little temperamental and that he'd get frustrated and agitated easily. We all figured that it was

150

mostly due to his inability to take care of himself and do the things that he used to do on his own and now couldn't. I knew that the PTSD and depression played a part in that also. Some days the nurse would come in to see that Willie had fallen out of the bed in his desperation to be independent and walk. Willie and I looked forward to the therapy sessions that we hoped and prayed would speed up his healing process.

After a few months of being at the facility, Willie was allowed to come home on some weekends for a few hours to visit. As soon as I found out that he could, I was very elated. I arranged and hired a private handicap van service to bring him home and pick him back up. Willie was so happy to see home again on his first visit. When he came home to visit, I usually called our neighbors over so they could visit with him. Willie was glad to see everyone.

One Sunday evening after our guests left, Willie asked me for the car keys so that he could go to the store and buy cigarettes. He could not drive, but he sure thought he could. This floored me because by this time, Willie had been sick for a few months and he hadn't had a cigarette. It seemed to me he would've quit automatically. I told him no and he tried his best to get out of the recliner. He tried so hard that he landed on the floor. Jamar could not get him up because he was too heavy for him to lift up off the floor. I ended up having to call the van to pick him up a couple of hours earlier than scheduled. I did not want him to stay on the floor too long.

When the van service came to pick him up and take him back to the nursing home, Willie asked me to give him some money just so he could have some on him. I gave it to him because I thought he might use some of it to give an extra tip to the driver.

I visited Willie the next day and I saw him sitting on the porch with another patient and their family members. I was shocked when I saw that Willie had spent his money on cigarettes. He was just smoking away. I asked him how in the world he got the cigarettes. He said that he gave the money to a patient's family member when they were on their way to the store. I blasted him about it. He then tried to make me feel guilty by saying that I was trying to take away the one thing that was giving him comfort and enjoyment. I encouraged him that he needed to quit smoking no matter how much comfort and joy it brought him because it could induce another stroke. He started stressing big time. He told me that he didn't care what happened. I knew right then that he said that out of anger and didn't really mean what he said.

I really wanted my husband to come home permanently, but at that time, our house couldn't accommodate his handicap needs. Willie was wheel chair bound. He would fall whenever he tried to get up on his own, even with a walker. All of the bedrooms are upstairs and all of the bathroom doors were too narrow for the wheelchair to get through. We started talking about purchasing a new house to be built with handicap accessibilities for Willie or finding one that was already handicapped equipped for him. Very soon, I started calling contractors, inquiring about the kind of house we needed to have. We had a couple of them to come out and talk with us. They started the long process in helping us.

One Monday, Willie told me that he wanted to be re-baptized again because he felt he needed a refreshing in his soul. He mentioned that he was first baptized as a teenager or in his early twenties. I didn't know how I was going to ask the church to do this and I was almost certain that it couldn't be done. I told Willie that it would probably be impossible because of his condition. He looked at me and said that all things were possible, just make the phone call.

I wasted no time. On Tuesday morning, I called our church and spoke with a young lady about the situation. She told me that she wasn't too sure that they could do it because of their liability clause. She told me that she would have the baptism department call me later on in the week.

I prayed to God that he would grant Willie's request. I received a call on Thursday morning from one of the deacons saying that he did not think that they could do it. My heart just fluttered and I just kept on praying because I did not want to have to tell Willie the church could not do it. Later that afternoon, I received a call from the head deacon, hoping that the call wasn't going to be a complete strike out. After we talked for a while pertaining to Willie's condition, he agreed to baptize Willie that coming Sunday. I couldn't believe he was willing to do it and do it so quickly. I was very excited to tell Willie. I asked him if he wanted to be baptized that quickly or did he want to wait a little longer since he knew the church would do it. He was fine with doing it right away. He said there was no need to wait around.

Sunday came and Willie was re-baptized. He was the first candidate that they put in the baptism pool. He was able to get his wish and people praised me because I was able to make it happen for him, with God's help. I thanked God gratefully. I was very elated to nurture my husband constantly with even the intangible things and pretty much did just about everything he asked of me during our lives together.

Shortly afterward, Willie expressed to me that he was tired of staying in that nursing/rehab facility because they were treating him too much like a baby. He wanted to be in a place where he could be more independent while waiting on our new house to be built. I was shocked when he told me that. I asked him where he would like to go, because I really didn't want him to leave there. I was very content with their service to him. He told me that he would even take a chance and go to the VA, even though he did not care too much for going there. All I could think of was that he wanted to be around more of a variety of his peers than that particular setting offered, and he needed a change. I wasted no time in getting him transferred because that was what he wished to do.

We were both impressed with their plan of care for him. They were somewhat advanced in some of their technology. They had a device that would pick up patients out of the bed and their wheelchairs that would carry them back and forth to the bathroom and for showers. I told Willie that was something that we needed to invest in when we moved into our new home. They gave Willie a reaching tool to use in order to pick up things off the floor while he was in the wheelchair or sitting on his bed. In Willie's mind, he continued to think that he could just get up out of the wheelchair by himself or out of the bed and just walk away, but he still couldn't do it.

One night, the nurse found Willie on the floor where he had slid down by the bed with his Bible in his hands. He told the nurse that he was trying to kneel down to read his Bible and pray. They got on him about that and told me to try and talk with him. I did, but I believe that Willie was doing just what his mind was signaling him to do. When I got after him about trying to get down on the floor to kneel and pray, he blurted out and told me that he was praying for God to deliver the devil out of me and he thought that God would hear his prayers quicker that way, on his knees. I replied that it appeared to me that the devil was more so in him and that he needed to do double praying for his own deliverance from it. He got mad with me and told me to shut up and not to say another word to him.

One day I went to visit Willie and noticed that his roommate's bed was empty and all of his belongings were gone. I thought he had gone home or something else had happened to him. I asked Willie about him. Willie told me that the staff transferred his roommate to another room because he had threatened to beat him up with his pick up/reaching tool device. Willie claimed that his roommate had put on his bedroom slippers and also took one of his t-shirts and was wiping down the windows in the room with it. I was really upset with Willie, but I decided to laugh the situation off. I told him that he probably should not have done that because his roommate probably did what he did by mistake. Willie asked me to leave him alone and if I cared so much about what happened, then I should go find the man and sleep with him if I wanted to.

As I was getting ready to leave that evening, Willie asked me to bring his car and park it outside. He also told me to bring his keys, wallet and cell phone. I told him that I wasn't going to bring those things because he couldn't drive and leave like some of the other patients who were in better condition than he was. He got angry and said that if I didn't do as I was told, he didn't want me to ever come see him again and to get out of his life completely.

When I went back to see him, Jamar was with me. I didn't have any of the items so I let Jamar go in ahead of me hoping that he wouldn't blow up at me if he saw his son's face first. When Jamar went in, Willie asked him where I was and Jamar said that I was by the door. I heard Willie telling him loudly that I better not step foot into his room if I didn't have the items. I came in and told him that I didn't have it and he turned violent on me. He picked up the reaching tool and hit me with it. At that moment, I wanted to take my walking cane and hit him back. I went outside the room with tears in my eyes, because I knew that he was just stressing and wanting to do things on his own and couldn't. He didn't want anyone telling him what he couldn't do.

Jamar just couldn't figure out what was going on with his dad, the reason why he was acting like that. One of the nurses tried to comfort Willie by telling him that he did not need any of his personal items in his room at all and definitely didn't need his car to just be parked outside because he couldn't drive it and that it was safer to be left at home. The nurse told us that she was going to note the

156

incident down so that his physician could review it and take further action. Willie told us that he did not need us to rule his life.

Immediately, upon receiving the information, the doctor placed Willie in anger management classes. A few days later, I went up to see Willie during one of his classes. The wheelchair assistant who wheeled him over to his class stopped me as I was headed that way. He told me that Willie was telling the whole staff that the reason why I didn't want to bring his items that he requested was because I must have been seeing another man, letting him drive his car and spending up his money. I told the assistant that none of what my husband accused me off was true.

My heart ached when he told me that. I had to sit down awhile to calm myself before I went to see Willie. When I got off the elevator to go to where Willie was, the security guard that was on duty came up to me and said the same thing. Tears came to my eyes as I tried to explain what was going on. I was elated when the guard asked if Willie suffered from PTSD or something to that nature. I told him yes and that his condition was severe. The guard told me that he pretty much understood why Willie was stressing and accusing me like that. He said that he knew of some people including family and friends who were suffering from PTSD. He understood that some of the behavior can be very erratic and they love to accuse others of everything they can think off. He said that PTSD was no joke. I felt a little better because somebody finally understood where I was coming from. I figured that if no one knew that Willie suffered from PTSD and understood the nature of the disease, they would believe everything he was saying about me.

A couple of days later, I came to the hospital; it appeared to me that the nurse's faces were shocked when they saw me come back. It seemed that they expected me to just stay away out of shame. And while it was true that I was ashamed, I wanted them all to see and know that I loved and cared for my husband despite his condition, his accusations, and his behavior. I was just hoping and praying that they had ignored the untruthful accusations about me and realized he said what he did because of stress.

One of the nurses stopped me before I got to Willie's room and told me that his doctor thought it would be best for Willie to be in a cessation program to help him quit the cigarette smoking. It sounded like a good idea to me, but he wouldn't sign up for it. I went on to Willie's room, but he wasn't there. I went to the patio where he and his buddies hung out. At that time, he was slowly wheeling himself out on the patio in the wheelchair sometimes using his right hand/arm. The smoke hovered around them as they puffed on their cigarettes like they were having a smoking contest. I looked at him and asked if he was trying to kill himself. I brought up the cessation program and he quickly said that he didn't want to participate. He looked at me and told me that I better not step foot toward him if I didn't have the items that he'd requested and if I got close to him, he was going to take my walking cane and knock me on my behind with it. I looked around at his friends; one of his friends had his wife there. I silently asked with my eyes if she was going through the same thing I was going through. She nodded slightly as if to say, "yes and I do understand."

I braced myself for the next words Willie spoke; he said that he was going to call someone to go pick up his stuff. He said that he was going to find someone who loved him. I told him that I loved him unconditionally. I asked him why in the world he asked to marry me. He took a puff of his cigarette and said that he thought he loved me then. With tears in my eyes, I placed money in his pocket pouch and left the building praying to God.

Chapter 14

A deacon from the church called my house to tell me that Willie called him asking could he come and take him to the bank. He told Willie that he couldn't do that unless he spoke to me about what was going on with the situation. The deacon revealed to me that my husband had been saying disparaging things about me. I wanted to tell him about my husband's condition, but somehow I felt that I would be slandering my husband and he probably wouldn't understand if I tried telling him.

I was getting tired of trying to tell people about PTSD, that Willie suffered from it, and explaining the symptoms of it. Sometimes I would try to tell people about the PTSD and they would ask me, what is that? I told the deacon the things Willie was saying were not true and that Willie was irritable and stressed because of his condition.

When I went back to the VA to see Willie, I saw that he was irritable. He told me that someone had stolen the money I had given him and he demanded that the staff call the police to file an incident report because there were crooks in the building. Willie said the police came and wrote up the incident. After the incident, I was on my way out of the VA when one of the nurses stopped me and apologized for what happened. I said no problem and kept on walking. I didn't want to know any more than what Willie had already told me. I was too ashamed to look her in the face. I was hoping that Willie didn't keep doing things to make the staff tired of him. However, after the incident, he didn't bother me about bringing his personal items in for him anymore.

When I came back to visit Willie, I had a few packs of chewing gum and some peppermints candy that I had purchased for him. As I was cleaning the empty gum and candy wrappers out of his bag in order to replenish it, I discovered the same money that he accused someone of stealing. It was right in the compartment where I put it. Willie apparently didn't search in there or he didn't remember that it was in there. I was speechless for a moment and then I showed it to Willie. He dropped his head in shame and said that he'd forgotten to check that compartment of the bag.

I was trying to figure out how I was going to tell the staff what we'd discovered, but Willie said that I needed to let him handle that. He said that he might not tell them anything, but even if he did, that would show the rest of the patients and staff there that nobody should ever mess with him.

The building contractors called me and said that they would be able to start building our new home in a few weeks. I was shocked when Willie told me that he wanted me to call them back to tell them that he didn't want to have the new house built. Instead, he told me to immediately get the contractors to come back over and see what they could do in remodeling our existing home and to add an additional room on with the handicap accessibilities that would accommodate him. When the contractors came back out, they told us that they could do the remodeling to add on the room and to also modify the inside of our home. They would be able to make the downstairs hallway wider, along with the utility bathroom, and the door downstairs so that Willie could move a little bit more freely in his wheelchair. I did what he asked without a moment's hesitation. Willie really didn't tell me why he changed his mind all of a sudden.

My next visit to see Willie, he started accusing me as soon as I stepped into his room door. He held up some toiletries from a hotel accusing me of bringing them there and placing them in his drawer for him to see that I was laying up with a man somewhere at the hotel and had the nerve to bring those souvenirs back for him. I tried to explain to him that I didn't bring those items and of course I wasn't messing around, for the trillionth time!

Willie realized that he stuck his foot in his mouth when he saw a nurse come in and put the exact items in his drawer while I was sitting there. When the nurse left out, all he could say was that he was sorry. God had that nurse to come in at the right time. The items were from various hotels that donated them to the nursing homes for the patients. In a way, I had become more and more used to Willie's constant accusations.

One morning, one of his therapists called me and said that they were planning to stop the therapy on Willie after another week or so because he hadn't made much progress with the paralysis on his left side. They said they had talked with him about it. I begged and pleaded that they keep the therapy going because it was Willie's desire to walk again.

162

They had extended his therapy once before for me. I told her if they stopped his therapy completely, he would probably give up on life because he looked forward to the days that he was scheduled to go. The head nurse told me that Willie and I had needed to face the facts and stop being in denial about Willie's condition. She said that Willie could stay in therapy for another two or three years and still remain in the same condition. She also said that I needed to face the fact that this is Willie's second stroke. The left side was already weakened from the first stroke eight months prior. She commented that I was an excellent wife to stick by and stand up for my husband and that I was a good advocate for him.

One Friday, one of the nurse case managers called and left a message on the house phone. I retrieved my calls while I was away from the house. It stated that Willie had signed release papers and he would be coming home on the van between 4:00 and 5:00p.m.

At that time, I felt helpless knowing that I could not take care of my husband like I wanted to. With a bad knee I could not do any lifting or pulling.

She continued to say on the message that they felt he was competent enough. I believed that it was only in his mind but not his body. I believed that Willie was just probably stressing to come home over petty stuff. It could have been that he knew he was not going to get any more therapy.

I called back and asked her if they were sending a nurse or some other kind of medical assistant to assist my husband in any way when he got home. She told me no.

163

After hanging up with her, I tried calling a couple of private health care offices out of the telephone directory, but I had no luck getting through to anyone that could possibly come out.

At that moment, I didn't know what else to do but to be home when he got there.

I called home to talk with Jamar. He had just got in from school. After telling him the news, he became panicky and hysterical. He asked how we'd take care of his dad. I told him that I didn't know and needed him to look out for the van that was bringing his dad home so he could open the door if they got to the house before I did. I knew I had to stop at the supermarket to get some other items that I thought Willie would need.

I was a few minutes away from the house when Jamar called and said that his dad was home and that I needed to hurry and get there because the van driver brought his dad home and left him outside in his wheelchair in the driveway near the garage per his dad's request and drove off. He was telling me that Willie had fallen out of his wheelchair onto the grass near the back yard fence trying to get through it to come to the back of the house. Willie got out of the chair thinking that he could walk. Jamar, only 13 years old, told me that he was able to get his dad back in the chair, even though he had difficulty doing so.

Willie had lost a lot of weight, but his body was like dead weight. As soon as I turned into our subdivision entrance, Jamar called me again, asking me where I was and to please hurry and get home in a frantic tone of voice. I asked him what happened. He said his dad had fallen out of the wheelchair again and he was not able to get him up.

164

When I turned into the driveway, I saw Willie lying down on the ground near the fence. I got out of the car and went over to where they were. Willie was scuffling, trying to get up, but he couldn't. He was soaking wet from the saturated ground due to the rain that had fallen the previous night and earlier that day.

I said, "Lord, please bless his soul", because it was so sad to see him like that and we couldn't do anything to help him. I told Willie that the only thing I could do was to call 911 for them to come and get him off the ground, because none of our men neighbors were home at that time to help us. Willie told me not to call 911. I told him that I was definitely going to do what I had to do and that was to call them, because he could not stay on that wet ground like that and end up being sick from it. As I was walking away to go inside to call 911, one of our neighbors drove up, came over and picked Willie up off the ground and placed him back in the wheelchair. Jamar pushed him into the house. I cannot imagine what would have happened if none of us were there when the van brought Willie home.

The only thing that Jamar and I could do at that moment was to just change his wet shirt. I knew that he had needed to be completely changed, so I called Willie's cousin and his wife who lived about ten minutes away from us to help me.

They came over immediately.

Chapter 15

My husband could maneuver his wheelchair independently a little with his right hand only. The first thing his cousins asked Willie was what he was thinking to sign himself out in the condition that he was in. They added that he knew that I couldn't do anything for him with my problematic knee except give him something to eat and make sure that he gets his medications. He started stressing and told them that he did not know and they must not ask him anything. They had a tough struggle trying to clean him up the best way they could for me, being that they could not get him in the bathroom. We discovered that the staff that sent Willie home didn't send any pampers along with him. They had been putting pampers on him at times but then letting him be independent at other times by letting him wear his regular underwear. He let them know when he had the urge and needed to go to the bathroom and they would come and bring the lifting equipment to pick him up and take him.

His cousin stopped cleaning him and went to the store and got a pack of pampers. I did not take any chances of letting them put regular underwear on him, even though Willie knew when he needed to use the bathroom, but the problem was getting to it. He couldn't do it by himself, and unfortunately we couldn't assist him. After they cleaned him, Willie wheeled himself to the kitchen table to eat and to take his meds.

All of a sudden as Willie was sitting at the kitchen table, he started throwing temper tantrums by running the wheelchair into the cooking range, dishwasher, kitchen sink cabinets, refrigerator and back over to the table. He picked up a glass of water and threw it at me, hitting me with it, all because we asked him the same question about why he signed out and the stress that came along with it, not being able to do anything by himself.

Seeing his behavior, they asked him why he was doing that. He said everything he could think of under the sun. His cousins asked me what I was going to do, because they didn't know what to tell me. I told them that I didn't know and couldn't even think at the moment. Before they left to go home, with intentions of coming back throughout the weekend to help Willie, they got him situated in the recliner in the living room so he could stretch out and sleep in it. As soon as they left, Willie took the recliner remote and tilted himself upward to get out thinking he could walk again and fell on the floor. I immediately called his cousin back over so he could put him back in the recliner. We moved the remote. I was so afraid of him injuring himself badly in his own house.

He wouldn't listen to me about his safety. The recliner was more comfortable for him to sit and relax in. I called around on Saturday inquiring if anyone knew of any private home care agencies. I asked Willie again if he realized what he'd done by coming home like this. He said no, he didn't realize it and that he was very sorry and did not mean to put pressure on us. He started to cry. My heart then weakened. I sort of figured that his motive for coming home was to make sure everything was being taken care of around the house, thinking that I could not do it. Willie didn't realize he couldn't do any better than I was doing. Every time he came home on visits, I would automatically show him a logbook on everything I spent. He never asked me to do it, but I wanted him to know.

The next day on that Sunday, I was able to contact a private home care worker, Ms. Meek. After telling her our situation, she told me that she could come early Monday morning to assess Willie's condition and our home in order to see what kind of care that she and her assistants could render to Willie.

Later on that Monday afternoon, I built up enough courage to ask Willie if he would be willing to do us both a favor by going back into the VA home until the house was ready in order for him to get the proper care. After asking that question, Willie agreed without putting up a fight that he would go back. I thanked the Lord, because I didn't want any more additional stress and frustration on him. I was also really concerned about his safety. I called back to the nursing home to speak with one of the head staff to see if Willie could come back and be placed on another floor under a new staff. I told her that my husband was willing. I was denied my petition. They told me that the only way Willie could come back is if he took sick for some reason that would require him to be transferred back there. She advised me to set up an appointment to see his primary care physician.

I hung up the phone and put my head down on the kitchen table in tears. I asked God to please come through once again for me because I didn't know what else to do. Moments later, my mind came across Ms. Coleman, a VA caseworker that Willie had seen briefly years ago just prior to him being diagnosed with PTSD. I called and told her everything that had happened with Willie. She requested to speak with Willie. After they spoke, she had deep sympathy for us and told him that he needed to try and calm his anger and stress level down and to stop hitting his wife. Willie told her that he was sorry that had happened and started to weep.

Ms. Coleman asked Willie if he realized his limitations before signing those discharge papers to release himself from the home. Willie told her that he wasn't too sure of what he was doing. She told us that she would help us. I needed to hear her say that. She wanted us to come in to her office that next day so she could discuss with us the help she was going to provide for Willie so he wouldn't have to stay at home in the condition he was in. After all, it would be a long period of time before we got our home in order. Willie told her that he did not realize anything. She had it set up where we would meet with his physicians briefly during the visit to her. The physicians also needed to see what Willie's feelings were about going back into another home.

I told Ms. Meek and her assistant that morning before they left our home, that it was a possibility that Willie would be going to another home soon, only temporarily and I would need them to come and assist him the best way they could until the time comes. I counted their help with Willie as a blessing.

Ms. Coleman immediately started the documentation process with the consent signature from Willie agreeing to go to another home. He made it clear to Ms. Coleman, that he didn't mind going, but he did not want to stay there more than three months. Ms. Coleman told Willie that she would work along with me and try hard to make that happen. She told us that he'd be eligible to stay in a private nursing facility along with the continuation of therapy since he could not go back to the VA. At that time, according to their policy when someone signed themselves out like Willie did, they could not go back.

That was all it took and what we wanted to hear! She was like an angel that God sent to help us in the most difficult time. She was willing to order a hospital bed to have delivered to the house while we waited for an available room for Willie at the home. Willie told us that there was no need for all of that right then because we knew that it was a possibility that he would be placed in a home soon. He stated if he had accepted one, the only place it could go was mainly in the living or dining room where we would have to take out some of the furniture. He said when the other room was completed; we would have enough space to put the bed in and could maneuver around better.

A couple of days later, Ms. Meek and her assistant did not show up at the house to assist Willie like we had talked about. I called her several times and left messages, but she would not return my calls. I really did not know what to think at that time, because I really needed Willie to be cleaned up. I figured she might have forgotten what we agreed on. Since they didn't show up and I couldn't get in touch, I had to call a cousin of mine to come over and help Willie.

Luckily, he was off from work that week and was willing to come back over throughout the remainder of the week and do the best he could. I continued to call Ms. Meek numerous times, but she never returned my calls. I began to think that they didn't want to come back because of Willie's condition and him being a difficult case to handle. I also think that they didn't believe our home was conducive to caring for Willie. From what I witnessed, they had a great struggle in assisting him. Even though they did not show up, by the grace of God, we had a little help while I continued to call around hoping to find another private home care service.

The next morning, I went upstairs to take a shower before my cousin came over. When I came back downstairs, Willie had already slid himself out of the recliner and landed on the floor and was dragging on his right side stating that he was trying to get up and walk in order to get to the bathroom. Willie suddenly started to cry and said that he needed to talk with his friend, Fred. I called Fred so they could talk. Fred told him that he needed to try and get a grip on things and to try to be a little more patient with all that is going on. He told Willie to stay put in the wheelchair, recliner, or whatever, rather than falling everywhere before he really banged himself up.

On that Sunday evening while we were at the table eating dinner, I saw Willie's mouth twisted to one side with his tongue hanging out, squeezing up his right fist to his

171

chest and his eyes rolling around and unresponsive. Jamar and I were very frightened to the point Jamar started screaming, jumping up and down and hitting the walls as I was dialing 911 and trying to talk and comfort Willie telling him, please do not leave us like that. It appeared to me that he was having another stroke and that one was taking him out. When the paramedics came, Willie became a bit more responsive. After I told the paramedics what had happened and that Willie was a stroke patient, they told me that they thought Willie had had a seizure. They said they see that often in some stroke patients and it was usually secondary to the stroke.

The paramedics took Willie on to the hospital where they kept him for two days. I was elated to know that it was only a seizure and that it's common in some stroke patients. I was also hopeful that he would get good rest in there, because he needed it. Willie was prescribed additional medications. I had never witnessed or experienced any one having a seizure attack like that one; even though Willie shook and gritted his teeth while sleeping at times. After that attack, I started thinking back to the day he was released to come home. I wondered if all of the stress that came with it caused him to have the seizure. Things didn't set well with me about that, so I got back in touch with his doctor at the nursing home to let her know what had been happening to my husband since the day of his release. I really wanted to know if there was a reason why Willie suddenly wanted to sign himself out in his condition.

She stated to me that Willie was crying and asking them to let him go home because he needed to take care of business. He told them that there was a money issue between him and me. I replied, a money issue! I told her that was not true. Willie and I never had a money issue as long as we have been together. She politely told me that was why he'd requested to come home and that they could not keep him.

I could only imagine how Willie had slandered my name and accused me of taking his money and personal belongings while he was there. After talking to her, it seemed to me that they had believed what Willie was saying about me and did not seem to realize that Willie was stressed and what frame of mind he was in. I felt so bad thinking that they probably believed those things Willie said about me. Besides his frame of mind, the only other reason I felt Willie would have brought up money issues and things needing to be done around the house, was because I mentioned to him one day that the car dealership wrote a letter stating that his car was due for service. The cost they quoted for the service was very high. He told me not to spend that much money to have it serviced. I told him that I would call around to see if I could find another dealer that would do it cheaper.

A lot of other things went out in the house that required a lot of money to be spent. The hot water heater and cooking range broke and were replaced with new ones. The clothes dryer also went out, but it was repaired. A lot of things went wrong while he was at the nursing home that I think might have prompted him to come home thinking he needed to be there. He was paranoid that people would rip me off and make me spend a lot of unnecessary money. I believe that he felt that he was the man of the house and that he should take care of those things like he always had. When he came home, the garbage disposal that he bought before he took sick was the only thing left undone that needed to be installed. While he was still home, we called the plumber to install it before he left to go to the other home. When he saw that I took care of all the other things, he was very pleased with it all and said that I had done an excellent job.

The weekend prior to Willie's leaving to go to the new nursing home; he mentioned to me that he really needed to get to the mall. I asked him why he needed to go there. He said that he needed to look for something that he could not find at the PX store in the VA hospital. He said that he had an assistant to wheel him there about three different times and they did not have it. I arranged to get him to the mall to fulfill his wishes. Jamar and I were with him. When Jamar wheeled him into Parisians Dept. Store, he almost fell over out the wheel chair when he saw my favorite perfume, and the one he liked me to wear (Red Door Velvet by Elizabeth Arden). He quickly bought the whole set for me, patted himself on the chest and said to the clerk that he was so happy that he was able to find his wife a birthday gift. After we left the store, we went to a seafood restaurant and had a lovely dinner.

Our cousins, the ones who were helping in assisting Willie since Ms. Meek never called me nor showed up, came over the night before he was to leave to assist Willie in getting ready for his transition from home to the new nursing facility. His personal barber came to the house to give him a haircut. I had hired Willie's personal barber to go to the nursing facilities to cut his hair per his request.

174

Willie seemed excited about going. It was truly a blessing that Willie would have his own private room at this home. I didn't want him to go, but I knew that it was really for the best in order for him to get the proper care and to cut down on his stress level for the time being.

When we got Willie to the nursing home, the therapist that evaluated him told us that he would do his best to get Willie up and walking. Willie looked up at the therapist and said, "I think I'm going to like him." They laughed together.

One of our cousins called me the next night and told me that while he had Willie outside talking the night before, Willie said that he was so sorry. He said Willie asked God to forgive him for being so hard on Jamar and me over the years. Willie claimed that his behavior and taking his frustrations out on us were simply due to his medical conditions. He said that he loved us so much and that I was strong and put up a great fight by sticking by his side through thick and thin. Willie had ended the conversation by telling him that I had passed the test in everything. I really didn't fully understand what it all meant, but I just kept encouraging my husband each and every day. Willie mentioned to him that he was so happy to have been able to stay at home for a while and to make sure things around the house were taken care of, because he thought I needed help.

Chapter 16

Willie's stay at the new private home seemed to be pleasant until he had a check up that startled both of us. Willie's prostate results came back abnormal. The doctor said that the abnormal test could be a result of an infection, enlarged prostate, an error, or cancer. It was my prayer to God asking that it be an error or an infection that could just be treated and cleared up. My heart began to flutter when I heard the word cancer. I asked the Lord to please not let anything else come upon my husband, because he probably wouldn't be able to handle anything else. Willie definitely did not want to hear that word cancer. He may have just asked God to just take him on home to Glory if he had to fight a battle with cancer in the condition that he was already in.

His doctor mentioned to us that he was going to refer Willie to a specialist (urologist) to have a scope done since his next lab report showed that it was still elevated. After the doctor talked about a scope needing to be done, Willie prayed that he didn't have cancer. He didn't want them sticking any kind of scope in him because it would hurt and he could not endure any more pain.

In October, a couple weeks before my birthday and after the prostate discussions, Willie started acting so nice and peaceful. Every time he saw me, he would greet me with his right arm open to a hug and he would say, "Hi, hon." He'd calmed his smoking habit down quite a bit and was chewing a lot of sugar free gum to help curb it completely. He met some patients in the home who he'd made friends with. They would be telling jokes and laughing a lot when they gathered outside on their breaks. They thought Willie was such a nice guy. Willie seemed to be coming along pretty well there.

On a Friday, I went to see Willie and I found him sleeping in his wheelchair. I scolded him about that and told him to ask a nurse to place him in the bed so that he could relax. He agreed with me and said that he would do that from then on.

As we were watching TV, all of a sudden, a solemn look came over Willie's face and he was staring me up and down. I caught him doing that a few times and asked him why he was staring at me like that and if something was wrong. He told me for no reason and that nothing was wrong. He wanted to thank me for everything that I had done for him including saving his life by giving him an aspirin before going to the hospital when he had that stroke that Sunday morning. He told me that I was a good, quick thinker to do that and thought it helped to prevent a blood clot from going to his brain. He said it could have been worse than it was.

I asked him why he was thanking me and he said because he wanted to. I asked him if he remembered our wedding vows when we both made them to be with each other during sickness and health until death do us part. He said he remembered. I told him that I was only fulfilling my

177

duties as a wife that I vowed and there was no need to thank me. I also said to him that I would continue to do so as long as God gives me the strength. I asked him to make sure that he prayed and asked God to give it to me. He told me not to worry because he always prays for his family and everyone else and that includes his enemies if he had any.

That night I had a dream about Willie. I dreamt that he was at a bank waiting on me to drive up to give him his bankcard. When I pulled into the parking lot, I saw Willie sitting in his car backed into a parking space with his eyeglasses on. I was praising him on how nice it was to see him finally driving again. He was so elated. Willie said that he knew I would be happy to see him up and driving. He told me he was going on a trip. He did not state where he was going. Somehow, I ended up in the car with him and I kept praising him about his ability to drive. I thought in my dreams that he was about to take a plane to wherever he was going, but when we arrived at our destination it was a ship terminal. I told Willie that I'd thought he was going on a plane. He told me no. I asked if he was going on that ship, he said yes with a peaceful and happy look on his face. Then he disappeared and I woke up.

I couldn't wait to tell Willie about my dream the next day, thinking that it was God's way of telling me that he was going to get better and be able to drive again and do other things for himself. Saturday morning, one of the contractors called me right before Jamar and I left to see Willie and told me that he needed to stop by to get another measurement for the room to be built. I waited until he came. Willie called me just prior to us leaving and asked me to bring him his favorite milkshake from Dairy Queen. I was about to leave the house when something dropped in my spirit and told me to get the olive oil that we use to anoint our foreheads with when we read the 23rd Psalm from the Bible. The oil was always placed on Willie's praying altar at home. Willie was the praying soldier of the house when he was in the right frame of mind. I felt that his prayers always kept us covered.

When Jamar and I got to Willie's room, he was lying on the bed and he told me that he asked the nurse to place him there so he wouldn't fall asleep in the chair like I had told him not to do. He asked me to call the nurse in again so that he could get up. As we waited for the nurse, I got the oil out and Willie's Bible that was in his drawer. Willie anointed his own forehead, I anointed his upper and lower extremities and we read the 23rd Psalm. He thanked me afterwards. When the nurse came in to get him up, I began telling him about the awesome dream I had of him the night before. The nurse and I were telling Willie that those were signs that God was going to heal him and get him out of his wheel chair. Willie became emotional and started crying. We asked him why he was crying. He said he didn't know why. I dried his tears and told him, please do not cry. I asked him if something was wrong. He said no.

Willie was speaking so nicely with Jamar. They watched a game on TV for a little while. Willie said that he wanted to go outside to get some fresh air. We went outside while Jamar decided to stay inside to watch TV. When Jamar and I were about to leave, Willie patted us on the backs and told me to bring him some spinach the next day, which was one of his favorite dishes. I told him I would.

When I arrived to see him on Sunday evening, he was in good spirits and ate very little of the spinach stating that he was still full from his dinner and that he did not want to get fat. I just smiled.

He looked at me and asked why I hadn't worn the perfume that he bought me because he did not smell it on me. I told him that I was waiting to open the kit for my birthday when we all go out to the restaurant to celebrate it on that upcoming Saturday. I had everything planned and arranged for us. I wanted to open it at the table and spray it on in front of him while he sang happy birthday to me. Willie said ok. Before I left his room that evening, I asked if he wanted me to call anyone so that he could talk to them. He told me that he wanted to talk to his brothers, his friend, Fred and a couple other family members. After Willie got through talking with them, he started to stare me down again. I couldn't figure out why he was doing it. I got a little worried, but didn't know why. I asked him again if there were something wrong and why he was staring at me the way he was. He then reassured me that there was nothing wrong. As I was about to get up from the side of his bed to leave, a piece of paper towel fell to the ground from his hand. As I was about to pick it up to put in the trashcan, Willie told me that he loved me very much and that he meant that from the depths of his heart.

He totally caught me by surprise because he hardly ever said that to me. It was really difficult for him to tell me that, but I knew for sure that he did love me unconditionally. I also knew that if I was in trouble and my husband had to walk across an ocean to get to me, he definitely would if he could, and I would do the same for him. I felt so good when he told me that. I went up to the wheelchair and landed a big kiss and a hug on him. I told him that he should know by now that I loved him for all that we have been through together. He said, "I know that."

I tilted his chin up with my fingers and looked him directly into his eyes and told him that whenever it was time for him to come home for good, I'd accept him with open arms, wheel chair or no wheel chair, walking or not walking and that I meant that from the depths of my heart. I assured him that I would get the best home care assistant for him that I possibly could. As I was leaving, he told me goodbye and said to make sure that I lock all the doors good when I got home.

I told Willie that I would see him the next day, which was Monday, near lunchtime after I stopped at the store to pick up a few things that he needed. When I got home, I sat down at the kitchen table to go through some paper work. Jamar was doing his homework. As we were sitting there, the phone rang, it was Willie calling, and it startled me because I'm the one who normally called him. I had just left there. The first thing I asked him was if something was wrong and if he was ok. Jamar was not with me at the home to see him because he had a lot of homework to finish. He asked if Jamar had finished his homework. I told him that he had and he asked to speak to Jamar. When they were speaking to each other, all I heard Jamar saying was "Yes, sir. Yes, sir. Yes sir." And when he was finishing the conversation, Jamar said, "I love you, too dad." It made me feel good to know that Willie had told Jamar that he loved him.

Jamar gave the phone back to me and Willie told me again that he loved me and reminded me to lock up the doors real good. I told him ok and that I loved him to and would see him tomorrow.

Monday, I stopped by the supermarket to pick up the items for Willie before going to him. As I was turning into a parking space at the store, my cell phone rang and it was one of the nurses calling to tell me that my husband had became a little ill and that they worked with him some, but had to have him transported by EMS to the hospital. At that moment, I did not have a chance to go into the store. I went straight to the hospital. I was very panicky and worried about what could possibly be wrong with my husband. The nurse did not tell me.

I arrived inside the hospital asking the front desk staff where my husband was. They told me to have a seat and they would get to me as soon as they finish helping the person that was ahead of me. I sat down very anxiously like I was on pins, hoping that it was something minor that caused him to fall ill, because he seemed to be perfectly fine on Sunday evening when I saw him. When it was my turn, the receptionist called me to come up so she could get insurance and other information from me for his admittance. I constantly asked her what he was transported there for. She said that when she got done, a nurse would come up and take me back to where my husband was and to see the doctor.

After finishing up at the front desk, a nurse came and got me and took me back through a double door into another waiting area until the doctor come in to talk with me about my husband. I was really prancing around with my walking cane with severe pain in my knee trying to peep in two of the rooms nearby to see if Willie was in one of them, but he wasn't. Finally, the doctor came in to see me. The first thing I asked him was, where was my husband and if he was all right. He asked me if the nurse who called me from the home mentioned to me that my husband suffered a heart attack while in therapy. I said, heart attack! I asked, how he was doing and if he needed surgery. Was he already in surgery or what? I asked how bad it was. The doctor said that he had a small pulse when he came, lost it and regained it, but then he lost it again. I asked the doctor in a frantic voice, what was he trying to tell me. The doctor looked at me and said that he was very sorry to tell me that they could not save my husband and he passed away.

At that moment, my whole body became numb and I felt like the whole world had came tumbling down upon me. I felt like my world had just ended and a dark cloud covered me over, causing me to feel lifeless and shattered. My eyes were so filled with tears that I could hardly see. I felt like my heart was ripped out and an empty hole was left there. I dropped down on the couch screaming and crying saying that it couldn't be true that my husband had gone and left me. The nurse was comforting me and told me to let her know when I was ready to go and view my husband's body. I was certainly in denial. He passed away before we could complete our plans to go out on Saturday and celebrate my birthday. He also hadn't had the chance to smell the perfume he bought for me one last time.

I finally gained a degree of strength and told the nurse that I was ready. When I stepped into the room and saw a white sheet over my husband, I broke down again and went out of the room. I had to fight to go back in to make sure that it was my husband. This time, I pulled the sheet back and it was Willie lying there lifeless. I cried louder, asking him why he left us. I asked God why he took my husband. I said to God that He could've at least extended my husband's life longer in order for him to come home permanently and enjoy living his life again at home. I wanted Willie to be able to take advantage of our remodeled home. I was saddened because he didn't have that chance.

I wanted the chance to show him that I was going to make sure he got the best care around. After I got my composure back a little, I called a family member that was home that day to come to the hospital to assist me and bring me home. I was devastated when asked which funeral home should come and pick up my husband's body. When we were leaving the hospital parking lot, I couldn't help but stare back at the hospital because I did not want to leave my husband there. I felt that he needed to come home with me. Lee met us at the house so we could tell Jamar.

When we told Jamar the news of his father's passing, he squeezed up his face extremely tight looking really devastated. I believe that his inner pain was so intense that he could not even shed a teardrop. I saw the pain on him. After telling him the news, Jamar would not talk with us the rest of the night. He went to his bedroom and became isolated from everyone. Jamar only attended his father's funeral, nothing else. I believe that if he could have gotten out of going to his father's funeral, he would have. It probably ripped a part of his little heart. Picking out the casket for Willie was another devastating thing to do. As I looked back over our lives together, I noticed that October was a significant month for us. October was the month we first met. It's also my birth month. Now it would be remembered as the month he passed away and was buried.

I believe that the lowest part of my life was the day of Willie's funeral. This was the same Saturday that we had planned to celebrate my birthday at the restaurant. I made sure that I sprayed some of the perfume on that day just for Willie. I believe that I went to great lengths to try and maintain a good relationship with him. I know we had our ups and downs, but for the most part I had Willie's heart and he had mine.

Now that I look back on everything, it's clear to me how God was preparing Jamar and I for Willie's departure. I didn't see it at first, but even with the baptism that he wanted done all of a sudden. It seems as if God allowed Willie to be sick and away from home so that Jamar and I could get used to him being gone forever. During the final weeks of Willie's life, it looked like God had made Willie act so nice and pleasant. He was more peaceful. I believe that the precious words we exchanged that Sunday evening, the day before he passed away, gave him a smooth sailing home and into eternity. It was just like my dream about him leaving to go on a ship where he was looking and sounding very happy. The way Willie acted in his final days near the end, made me feel that he felt the end was drawing near, or he knew that his time was up here on earth.

It took great courage; wisdom, kindness, strength, and most of all, love and patience to get me through my years with Willie. I know that God's grace, favor, peace, and power were given to me so that I would not lose courage under the pressure. God's strength made it possible for me to be Willie's anchor and his inward supporter and to help him in balancing his life through all of his struggles. I am so happy that I was able to always stand by my husband's side and defend him as well. On this journey, I have also encountered God's faithfulness and His gentle Spirit.

I believe that God placed me in Willie's life, regardless of the situation, so that I could be the driving force in his life and to let him know how much we loved him. I also believe that God placed me in Willie's life to help him through a battle he would have never won on his own.

No matter what kind of situations we go through in life, God's help is always there to restore and to elevate us.

We love and miss you, Willie.

PTSD Information

Dr. Knight gave us a pamphlet, titled the READJUSTMENT PROBLEMS AMONG VIETNAM VETERANS: The Etiology of Combat-Related Post-Traumatic Stress Disorders. By Jim Goodwin, Psy.D. Published by Disabled American Veterans, National Headquarters, P.O. Box 14301, Cincinnati, OH 45214 (vv-2)

She hoped that the information would give us a better understanding of what some of the veterans went through on the battlefield at war and some of their symptoms afterwards. Of Course, Willie did not want any part in reading it and didn't want to know what was in it. I certainly wanted to know. I brought it home and read through it. The information in that pamphlet follows:

Introduction: Most Vietnam veterans have adjusted well to life back in the United States, following their wartime experiences. That's a tribute to these veterans who faced a difficult homecoming to say the least.

However, a very large number of veterans haven't made it all the way home from the war in Southeast Asia. By conservative estimates, at least half a million Vietnam veterans still lead lives plagued by serious, war-related readjustment problems. Such problems crop up in a number of ways, varying from veteran to veteran, Flashbacks to combat, feelings of alienation or anger... depression, loneliness and an inability to get close to others...Sometimes drug or alcohol problems...perhaps even suicidal feelings. The litany goes on.

The material presented here is a condensation of Dr. Goodwin's chapter in Post-Traumatic Stress Disorders of the Vietnam Veteran: Observations and Recommendations for the Psychological Treatment of the Veteran and His Family. It is hoped that Dr. Goodwin's paper will provide all of the information on post-traumatic stress disorders needed by veterans, their families, and the general public.

Edited by Tom Williams, Psy.D, this book was published by the nonprofit Disabled American Veterans as a guide to counseling professionals who are working with or interested in the problems of Vietnam veterans. Due to limited quantities, the complete book has made available chiefly to psychiatrists, psychologists and other mental health and counseling professionals.

RECOLLECTIONS: *Skypeck, George L. Captain, (1971). U.S.A p.3*

What price must the heart pay to live and love? Say you long hot days ahead without a kind word---days when fear will tear your insides apart—but one must go for duty calls...so very far away. My heart is numb, my brain reels---yet no tears. Another friend is laid to rest. God rest his soul this brave man. Keep him safe for we'll meet again---at another time, in another place. Hot sun, endless hours grant me some respite from loneliness.

Sharp rattles of orange streaks across the black sky--- a sensation of torn steel woven with hot flesh and blood beside me. God! God, whatever God you be, speed my soul on its way but not in endless eternity. Thoughts of home come to me; don't let me go; please no—I'm afraid!

A cold refreshing wind penetrates my bones---what a strange place this is. I hear familiar voices that have long passed from existence---I see faces of friends long since dead. I realize now what has happened and where I am; yet I am happy with those whose names are carved in stone amidst the grass of a place called Arlington.

Please don't weep for me for I no longer worry about what tomorrow brings...for me it brings a much-needed rest...a rest forever.

One veteran goes on to say, "My marriage is falling apart. We just don't talk any more. Hell, I guess we've never really talked about anything, ever. I spend most of my time at home alone in the basement. She's upstairs and I'm downstairs. Sure we'll talk about the groceries and who will get gas for the car, but that's about it. She tries to tell me she cares for me, but I get real uncomfortable talking about things like that and I get up and leave. Sometimes I get real angry over the smallest thing. I used to hit her when this would happen, but lately I just punch out a hole in the wall, or leave and go for a long drive. Sometimes I spend more time on the road just driving aimlessly than I do at home.

"I really don't have any friends and I'm pretty particular about who I want as a friend. The world is pretty much dog eating dog and no one seems to care much for anyone else. As far as I'm concerned, I'm really not a part of this messed up society. What I'd really like to do is have a home in the mountains, somewhere far away from everyone. Sometimes I get so angry about the way things are being run. I think about placing a few blocks of C-4 (military explosive) under some of the sons-of-bitches. A couple of times a year, I get into fights at bars. I usually pick the biggest guy. I don't know why, I usually get creamed. There are times when I drive real crazily, screaming and yelling at other drivers.

"I usually feel depressed. I've felt this way for years. There have been times I've been so depressed that I won't even leave the basement. I'll usually start drinking pretty heavily around these times. I've also thought about committing suicide when I've been depressed. I've got an old .38 that I snuck back from Nam. A couple of times, I've sat with it loaded, once I even had the barrel in my mouth and the hammer pulled back. I couldn't do it. I see Smitty back in Nam with his brains smeared all over the bunker. Hell, I fought too hard then to make it to the World (U.S.); I can't waste it now. How come I survived and he didn't? There has to be some reason.

"Sometimes, my head starts to replay some of my experiences in Nam. Regardless of what I'd like to think about, it comes creeping in. It's so hard to push back out again. Its old friends, their faces, the ambush, the screams, their faces (tears)...You know, every time I hear a chopper (helicopter) or see a clear unobstructed green tree line, a chill goes down my back; I remember. When I go hiking now, I avoid green areas. I usually stay above timberline. When I walk down the street, I get real uncomfortable with people behind me that I can't see. When I sit, I always try to get a chair with something big and solid directly behind me. I feel most comfortable in the corner of a room, with walls on both sides of me. Loud noises irritate me and sudden movement or noise will make me jump.

"Night is hardest for me. I go to sleep long after my wife has gone to bed. It seems like hours before I finally drop off. I think of so many of my Nam experiences at night. Sometimes my wife awakens me with a wild look in her eye. I'm all sweaty and tense. Sometimes I grab for her neck before I realize where I am. Sometimes I remember the dream; sometimes it's Nam, other times its just people after me, and I can't run anymore. "I don't know; this has been going on for so long; it seems to be getting gradually worse. My wife is talking about leaving. I guess it's no big deal. But I'm lonely. I really don't have anyone else. Why am I the only one like this? What the hell is wrong with me?"

The above description of one Vietnam veteran's problematic lifestyle, many years after the war in Southeast Asia, is unfortunately not an unusual phenomena.

The Evolution of Post-Traumatic Stress Disorder: It was not until World War I that specific clinical syndromes came to be associated with combat duty. In prior wars, it was assumed that such casualties were merely manifestations of poor discipline and cowardice. However, with the protracted artillery barrages commonplace during "The Great War, " the concept evolved that the high air pressure of the exploding shells caused actual physiological damage, precipitating the numerous symptoms that were subsequently labeled "shell shock." By the end of the war, further evolution accounted for the syndrome being labeled a "war neurosis" (Glass, 1969).

The Symptoms of Post-Traumatic Stress Disorder: Chronic and/or Delayed. (Depression). The Vast majority of the Vietnam combat veterans I have interviewed are depressed. Many have been continually depressed since their experiences in Vietnam. They have the classic symptoms (DMS 111, 1980) of sleep disturbance, psychomotor retardation, feelings of worthlessness, difficulty in concentrating, etc. Many of these veterans have weapons in their possession, and they are no strangers to death. In treatment, it is especially important to find out if the veteran keeps a weapon in close proximity, because the possibility of suicide is always present.

When recalling various combat episodes during an interview, the veteran with post-traumatic stress disorder almost invariably cries. He usually has had one or more episodes in which one of his buddies was killed. When asked how he handled these deaths when in Vietnam, he will often answer in the shortest amount of time possible" (Howard, 1975). Due to circumstances of war, extended grieving on the battlefield is very unproductive and could become a liability. Hence, grief was handled as quickly as possible, allowing little or no time for the grieving process.

Many men reported feeling numb when this happened. When asked how they are now dealing with the deaths of their buddies in Vietnam, they invariably answer that they are not. They feel depressed; "How can I tell my wife, she'd never understand?" they ask. "How can anyone who hasn't been there understand?" (Howard, 1975).

Accompanying the depression is very well developed sense of helplessness about one's condition. Vietnam-style combat held no final resolution of conflict for anyone. Regardless of how one might respond, the overall outcome seemed to be just an endless production of casualties with no perceivable goals attained. Regardless of how well one worked, sweated, bled and even died, the outcome was the same. Our GIs gained no ground; they were constantly rocketed or mortared. They found little support from their "friends and neighbors" back home, the people in whose name so many were drafted into military service. They felt helpless. They returned to the United States, trying to put together some positive resolution of this episode in their lives, but the atmosphere at home was hopeless. They were still helpless. Why even bother anymore?

"Many veterans report becoming extremely isolated when they are especially depressed. Substance abuse is often exaggerated during depressive periods. Self-medication was an easily learned coping response in Vietnam' alcohol appears to be the drug of choice.

Isolation: Combat veterans have few friends, many veterans who witnessed traumatic experiences complain of feeling like old men in young men's bodies. They feel isolated and distant from their peers. The veterans feel that most of their non-veteran peers would rather not hear what the combat experience was like; therefore they feel rejected. Much of what many of these veterans had done during the war would seem like horrible crimes to their civilian peers. But, in the reality faced by Vietnam combatants, such actions were frequently the only means of survival.

Many veterans find it difficult to forget the lack of positive support they received from the American public during the war. This was especially brought home to them on the return from the combat zone to the United States. Many were met by screaming crowds and the media calling them "depraved fiends" and "psychopathic killers" (DeFazio, 1978). Many personally confronted hostility from friends and family, as well as strangers. After their return home, some veterans found that the only defense was to search for a safe place. These veterans found themselves criss-crossing the continent, always searching for that place where they might feel accepted. Many veterans cling to the hope that they can move away from their problems. It is not unusual to interview a veteran who, either alone or with his family, has effectively isolated himself from others by repeatedly moving from one geographical location to another. The stress on his family is immense.

The veteran will often stay in the house and avoid any interactions with others. He also resents any interactions that his spouse may initiate. Many times, the wife is the source of financial stability.

Rage: The veterans' rage is frightening to them and to others around them. For no apparent reason, many will strike out at whomever is near. Frequently, this includes their wives and children. Some of these veterans can be quite violent. This behavior generally frightens the veterans, apparently leading many to question their sanity; they are horrified at their behavior. However, regardless of their afterthoughts, the rage reactions occur with frightening frequency.

Often veterans will recount episodes in which they became inebriated and had fantasies that they were surrounded or confronted by enemy Vietnamese. This can prove to be an especially frightening situation when others confront the veteran forcibly. For many combat veterans, it is once again a life-and-death struggle, a fight for survival.

Some veterans have been able to sublimate their rage, breaking inanimate objects or putting fists through walls. Many of them display bruises and cuts on their hands. Often, when these veterans feel the rage emerging, they will immediately leave the scene before somebody or something gets hurt; subsequently, they drive about aimlessly. Quite often, their behavior behind the wheel reflects their mood. A number of veterans have described to me the verbal catharsis they've achieved in explosions of expletives directed at any other drivers who may wrong them.

There are many reasons for the rage. Military training equated rage with masculine identity in the performance of military duty (Eisenhart, 1975). Whether one was in combat or not, the military experience stirred up more resentment and rage than most had ever felt (Egendorf, 1975). Finally, when combat in Vietnam was experienced, the combatants were often left with wild, violent impulses and no one upon whom to level them. The nature of guerrilla warfare---with its use of such tactics as booby trap land mines and surprise ambushes with the enemy's quick retreat---left the combatants feeling like time bombs; the veterans wanted to fight back, but their antagonists had long since disappeared. Often they unleashed their rage at indiscriminate targets for want of more suitable targets (Shatan, 1978).

Avoidance of feelings: Alienation: The spouses of many veterans I have interviewed complain that the men are cold, uncaring individuals, indeed, the veterans themselves will recount episodes in which they did not feel anything when they witnessed the death of a buddy in combat or the more recent death of a close family relative. They are often somewhat troubled by these responses to tragedy; but, on the whole, they would rather deal with tragedy in their own detached way.   What becomes especially problematic for these veterans, however, is an inability to experience the joys of life. They often describe themselves as being emotionally dead (Shatan, 1973).

Many veterans find it extremely uncomfortable to feel love and compassion for others. To do this, they would have to thaw their numb reactions to the death and horror that surrounded them in Vietnam. Some veterans I've interviewed actually believe that if they once again allow themselves to feel, they may never stop crying or may completely lose control of themselves; what they mean by this is unknown to them. Therefore, many of these veterans go through life with an impaired capacity to love and care for others. They have no feeling of direction or purpose in life. They are not sure why they even exist.

Survival Guilt: When others have died and some have not the survivors often ask, "How is it that I survived when others more worthy than I did not?" (Lifton, 1973). Survival guilt is an especially guilt-invoking symptom. It is not based on anything hypothetical. Rather, it is based on the harshest of realities, the actual death of comrades and the struggle of the survivor to live. Often the survivor has had to compromise himself or the life of someone else in order to live. The guilt that such an act invokes or guilt over simply surviving may eventually end in self-destructive behavior by the survivor. Many veterans, who have survived when comrades were lost in surprise ambushes, protracted battles or even normal battlefield attrition, exhibit self-destructive behavior. It is common for them to recount the combat death of someone they held in esteem; and, invariably, the question comes up, "Why wasn't it me?"

Anxiety Reactions: Many Vietnam veterans describe themselves as very vigilant human beings; their autonomic senses are tuned to anything out of the ordinary. A loud discharge will cause many of them to start. A few will actually take such evasive action as falling to their knees or to the ground. Many veterans become very uncomfortable when people walk closely behind them. One veteran described his discomfort when people drive directly behind him. He would pull off the road, letting others pass when they got within a few car lengths of him.

Some veterans are uncomfortable when standing out in the open. Many are uneasy when sitting with others behind them, often opting to sit up against something solid, such as a wall. The bigger the object is, the better. Many combat veterans are most comfortable when sitting in the corner in a room, where they can see everyone about them. Needless to say, all of these behaviors are learned survival techniques. If a veteran feels continuously threatened, it is difficult for him to give such behavior up.

A large number of veterans possess weapons. This also is a learned survival technique. Many still sleep with weapons in easy reach. The uneasy feeling of being caught asleep is apparently very difficult to master once having left the combat zone.

Sleep Disturbance and Nightmares: Few veterans struggling with post-traumatic stress disorders find the hours immediately before sleep very comfortable. In fact, many will stay awake as long as possible. They will often have a drink or smoke some cannabis to dull any uncomfortable cognition that may enter during this vulnerable time period. Many report that they have nothing to occupy their minds at the end of the day's activities, and their thoughts wander. For many of them, it is a trip back to the battle zone. Very often they will watch TV late into the mornings.

Finally, with sleep, many veterans report having dreams about being shot at or being pursued and left with an empty weapon, unable to run anymore. Recurrent dreams of specific traumatic episodes are frequently reported. It is not unusual for a veteran to re-experience, night after night, the death of a close friend or a death that he caused as a combatant. Dreams of everyday, common experiences in Vietnam are also frequently reported. For many, just the fear that they might actually be back in Vietnam is very disquieting.

Some veterans report being unable to remember their specific dreams, yet they feel dread about them. Wives and partners report that the men sleep fitfully, and some call out in agitation. A very few actually grab their partners and attempt to do them harm before they have fully awakened.

Finally, maintaining sleep has proven to be a problem for many of these veterans. They report waking up often during the night for no apparent reason. Many rise quite early in the morning, still feeling very tired.

Intrusive Thoughts: Traumatic memories of the battlefield and other less affect-laden combat experiences often play a role in the daytime cognitions of combat veterans. Frequently, these veterans report replaying especially problematic combat experiences over and over again. Many search for possible alternative outcomes to what actually happened in Vietnam. Many castigate themselves for what they might have done to change the situation, suffering subsequent guilt feelings to day because they were unable to do so in combat. The vast majority reports that these thoughts are very uncomfortable, yet they are unable to put them to rest.

Many of the obsessive episodes are triggered by common everyday experiences that remind the veteran of the war zone; helicopters flying overhead, the smell of urine (corpses have no muscle tone, and the bladder evacuates at the moment of death), the smell of diesel fuel (the commodes and latrines contained diesel fuel and were burned when filled with human excrement), green tree lines (these were searched for any irregularity which often meant the presence of enemy movement), the sound of popcorn popping (the sound is very close to that of small arms gunfire in the distance), any loud discharge, a rainy day (it rains for months during the monsoons in Vietnam) and finally the sight of Vietnamese refuges.

Other sources of information on Vietnam Veterans and PTSD can be found online at www.vietvet.org/ptsdinfo.htm and www.patiencepress.com/patience_press/PTSD_Help-For.Kids.html
Patience Mason is the author of the small book entitled "Why Is Daddy Like He Is?" The information can be found on her website at the link above.

If you have enjoyed reading this book, please consider leaving a review on Amazon or signing the guest book on my website.
www.thewilliegraystory.com

Thank you and May God Bless